The Quantum Revolution

How Tomorrow's Computers Will Transform Our World

By Douglas Donovan

IBSN: 979-8-3302-7592-2

Preface

In a bustling conference room in Silicon Valley, I found myself caught between two dramatically different conversations about the same technology. On one side, a venture capitalist was breathlessly explaining how quantum computers would solve climate change, cure cancer, and revolutionize artificial intelligence within the next five years. On the other side, a quantum physicist was patiently explaining why we're still decades away from practical quantum computers that can outperform classical systems for most real-world problems.

Both were talking about quantum computing, yet they might as well have been discussing entirely different technologies.

This paradoxical situation captures the essence of where we stand today with quantum computing. The technology exists in a strange superposition of its own—simultaneously revolutionary and nascent, promising and overhyped, transformative and still largely theoretical. Like the quantum particles that power these machines, quantum computing seems to exist in multiple states at once: it's both the future of computation and a technology still struggling with basic engineering challenges.

The truth, as often happens, lies somewhere between these extremes. Quantum computing represents one of the most significant technological paradigm shifts in human history, comparable to the invention of the transistor or the development of the internet. However, this revolution won't happen overnight, and it won't solve every problem we throw at it. Understanding the reality of quantum computing—its genuine capabilities, current limitations, and future potential—has never been more important.

Why This Book Matters Now

We stand at a critical juncture in the development of quantum technology. The first generation of quantum computers has moved from research laboratories into commercial cloud services. Companies like

IBM, Google, and Amazon offer quantum computing access to anyone with an internet connection. Major corporations are investing billions of dollars in quantum research, and governments around the world are launching national quantum initiatives with funding that reaches into the tens of billions.

Yet despite this massive investment and growing availability, quantum computing remains shrouded in mystery for most people. The physics underlying these machines seems to defy common sense, leading to explanations that either oversimplify the technology into science fiction or overwhelm readers with mathematical complexity.

This book bridges that gap. You don't need a physics degree to understand quantum computing's impact on our world. Just as you don't need to understand how transistors work to use a smartphone effectively, you don't need to master quantum mechanics to grasp how quantum computers will transform industries, threaten current security systems, and create entirely new categories of problems we can solve.

What You'll Discover

This book will take you on a journey from the bizarre world of quantum mechanics to the practical realities of building quantum computers. You'll discover how these machines leverage the strange properties of quantum particles—like existing in multiple states simultaneously or being mysteriously connected across vast distances—to perform calculations that would take classical computers longer than the age of the universe.

We'll explore the heated global competition for quantum supremacy, where nations and corporations race to build more powerful quantum systems. You'll learn about the current state of quantum technology, including its significant limitations and the engineering challenges that researchers face daily. Most importantly, you'll understand how quantum computing will impact your life, from the security of your online banking to the development of new medicines that could save millions of lives.

The book also confronts the darker implications of quantum technology. Current encryption methods that protect everything from your credit card information to national security secrets will become vulnerable to quantum attacks. Cryptocurrencies like Bitcoin face an existential threat. We'll examine how governments, corporations, and individuals are preparing for this quantum disruption.

A Balanced Perspective

This book aims to provide a realistic assessment of quantum computing—neither dismissing it as overhyped nor accepting every bold prediction about its transformative power. The field is filled with genuine breakthroughs and legitimate excitement, but it's also plagued by misconceptions, premature claims, and unrealistic timelines.

By the end of this book, you'll be equipped to cut through the hype and understand what quantum computing can and cannot do. You'll recognize the genuine game-changing applications while maintaining healthy skepticism about grandiose claims. Most importantly, you'll understand how to prepare for a world where quantum computers are not just laboratory curiosities, but essential tools shaping our economy, security, and daily lives.

The quantum revolution is not coming—it has already begun. The question is not whether quantum computers will transform our world, but how quickly and in what ways. This book will help you understand both the opportunities and challenges ahead, ensuring you're prepared for the quantum age that's rapidly approaching.

Chapter 1: The Quantum Puzzle - Understanding the Impossible

Imagine you're standing at a fork in the road, trying to decide which path to take. In the classical world we're familiar with, you must choose one path or the other. You can't walk down both simultaneously. Now imagine a traveler who could somehow explore both paths at the same time, experiencing every possible journey before deciding which route leads to the best destination. This impossible scenario captures the essence of how quantum computers process information—they can explore multiple solutions simultaneously, finding answers to problems that would take classical computers millennia to solve.

This isn't science fiction. This is the foundation of quantum computing, a technology that harnesses some of the most counterintuitive phenomena in physics to revolutionize how we process information. To understand why quantum computers represent such a dramatic leap forward, we must first examine the limitations of classical computing and then venture into the strange world where quantum mechanics meets computer science.

The Classical Computing Wall

Every smartphone in your pocket, every laptop on your desk, and every supercomputer in research facilities around the world operates on the same fundamental principle established by computer pioneers in the 1940s. They process information using bits—binary digits that can be either 0 or 1, representing "off" or "on" states in electronic circuits. These bits combine to represent more complex information: your text messages, photos, videos, and the software that runs your favorite applications.

Classical computers have become extraordinarily powerful through miniaturization and engineering excellence. Modern processors contain billions of transistors, each smaller than viruses, switching on and off billions of times per second. This incredible density and speed have driven the exponential improvements in computing power that we've witnessed over the past fifty years, often summarized by Moore's Law—

the observation that computer processing power doubles approximately every two years.

However, this approach to computing faces fundamental limitations that no amount of engineering brilliance can overcome. Certain types of problems require so many calculations that even the most powerful classical computers would need longer than the age of the universe to solve them. These aren't esoteric mathematical curiosities—they're practical problems that could revolutionize medicine, energy, and our understanding of the universe itself.

The Factoring Challenge

Consider the seemingly simple problem of factoring large numbers. If someone gives you the number 15 and asks you to find its factors, you can quickly determine that $15 = 3 \times 5$. But what if someone gives you a number with 300 digits and asks for its factors? For classical computers, this becomes an almost impossible task.

This difficulty isn't just a mathematical curiosity—it's the foundation of modern internet security. Every time you make an online purchase or send a private message, your information is protected by encryption systems that rely on the fact that factoring large numbers is computationally infeasible for classical computers. The security of our digital world depends on certain problems being too difficult for classical computers to solve quickly.

The Molecular Modeling Dilemma

Another limitation emerges when we try to understand complex molecular systems. A caffeine molecule contains just 24 atoms, but accurately modeling its quantum properties requires tracking an astronomical number of possible states. As molecules grow larger, the computational requirements increase exponentially. Understanding how proteins fold—a process crucial for drug discovery—requires modeling molecules with thousands of atoms. The computational resources needed grow so rapidly that classical computers cannot handle molecules of practical interest for pharmaceutical research.

These limitations aren't temporary obstacles that better engineering will overcome. They're fundamental constraints imposed by the nature of classical computation itself. Even if we could build classical computers the size of planets, using every atom as a computational element, we still couldn't solve certain problems in reasonable timeframes.

Enter the Quantum Advantage

Quantum computers approach these challenges from an entirely different angle. Instead of processing information with classical bits that must be either 0 or 1, quantum computers use quantum bits—qubits—that can exist in multiple states simultaneously. This isn't merely a minor improvement in how we store information; it represents a fundamental shift in the nature of computation itself.

When a classical computer examines a problem with many possible solutions, it must check each possibility one by one, like a person methodically trying every key on a keyring to find the one that opens a lock. A quantum computer, by contrast, can examine many possibilities simultaneously, as if the lock could somehow try multiple keys at once and identify the correct one directly.

The Power of Superposition

The source of quantum computing's power lies in a quantum mechanical phenomenon called superposition. In the quantum world, particles can exist in multiple states simultaneously until they're measured or observed. A quantum bit can be in state 0, state 1, or any combination of both states at the same time. This isn't just theoretical—it's a measurable physical phenomenon that quantum computers exploit for computational advantage.

To understand how dramatic this advantage can be, consider what happens as we add more qubits to a quantum system. Two classical bits can represent one of four possible states: 00, 01, 10, or 11. At any given moment, those two bits must be in exactly one of these states. Two qubits, however, can exist in a superposition of all four states simultaneously. Three qubits can represent all eight possible combinations of three bits, four qubits can represent sixteen combinations, and so forth.

The scaling becomes extraordinary quickly. While 300 classical bits can represent just one of 23002300 possible states at any given time, 300 qubits can represent all 23002300 states simultaneously. This number is larger than the estimated number of atoms in the observable universe. This exponential scaling gives quantum computers their theoretical power to solve certain problems exponentially faster than classical computers.

The Entanglement Advantage

Superposition alone doesn't provide quantum computers with their full power. The second crucial quantum phenomenon is entanglement—a mysterious connection between quantum particles that Albert Einstein famously called "spooky action at a distance." When qubits become entangled, measuring one qubit instantly affects the state of its entangled partners, regardless of how far apart they are.

For quantum computing, entanglement serves as a computational resource that allows qubits to work together in ways that classical bits cannot. Entangled qubits can process information collectively, performing coordinated operations that would require complex communication networks in classical systems. This cooperative behavior enables quantum algorithms to solve certain problems with fewer computational steps than any known classical algorithm.

What Makes Quantum Computing Different

Understanding quantum computing requires abandoning some of our most basic intuitions about how information processing works. In classical computing, information flows in predictable, deterministic ways. Give a classical computer the same input twice, and it will always produce the same output. The internal state of the computer at any moment can, in principle, be completely known and predicted.

Quantum computers operate under fundamentally different rules. They process information probabilistically, meaning that running the same quantum program multiple times may produce different results. This isn't a flaw in the system—it's an inherent feature of quantum mechanics that quantum computers leverage for computational advantage.

Probabilistic vs. Deterministic Processing

When a quantum computer solves a problem, it doesn't guarantee the correct answer on every run. Instead, it produces the correct answer with high probability. Quantum algorithms are designed to increase the likelihood of measuring the correct result while decreasing the probability of measuring incorrect answers. This might seem like a disadvantage, but for many problems, getting the right answer with 99% certainty after a few minutes is far superior to getting a guaranteed answer after waiting millions of years.

This probabilistic nature requires a different approach to algorithm design. Classical algorithms follow deterministic steps: do this, then this, then this, and you'll get the answer. Quantum algorithms involve preparing quantum states, manipulating them through quantum operations, and then measuring the results to extract information. The art of quantum algorithm design lies in choreographing these quantum operations so that the desired answer has the highest probability of appearing when measurements are made.

Parallel Processing Beyond Classical Limits

Classical computers can achieve parallelism by running multiple processors simultaneously, but they're limited by physical constraints. Even the most powerful supercomputers have finite numbers of processors, and communication between processors introduces delays and complexity.

Quantum computers achieve a different kind of parallelism through superposition. A single quantum processor can, in effect, perform calculations on all possible inputs simultaneously. This isn't just faster parallel processing—it's a qualitatively different computational model that allows quantum computers to solve certain problems exponentially faster than any classical computer, regardless of how many classical processors work together.

The Measurement Problem

One of the most challenging aspects of quantum computing involves extracting useful information from quantum calculations. While qubits can exist in superposition states during computation, measuring them causes them to "collapse" into definite 0 or 1 states. This measurement process destroys the superposition that gave the quantum computer its computational advantage.

This creates a delicate balance in quantum algorithm design. The algorithm must manipulate quantum states to encode the solution to a problem, but it must do so in a way that allows useful information to be extracted through measurement. Clever quantum algorithms find ways to amplify correct answers and diminish incorrect ones, so that measurement yields useful results despite the inherent randomness of quantum mechanics.

The Quantum Mechanics Foundation

To truly appreciate quantum computing's revolutionary potential, we need to understand the quantum mechanical phenomena that make it possible. Quantum mechanics governs the behavior of matter and energy at the smallest scales, describing a world that operates according to fundamentally different rules than our everyday experience.

Wave-Particle Duality

In the quantum world, particles exhibit properties of both waves and particles, depending on how they're observed. This dual nature allows quantum systems to exhibit interference effects—where different quantum states can strengthen or cancel each other out, similar to how sound waves can amplify or silence each other when they meet.

Quantum computers exploit interference effects to amplify correct answers while canceling out incorrect ones. By carefully designing quantum algorithms, engineers can ensure that wrong answers interfere destructively (canceling each other out) while correct answers interfere constructively (reinforcing each other). This selective amplification allows quantum computers to find solutions to problems buried among exponentially large numbers of possibilities.

The Uncertainty Principle

Werner Heisenberg's uncertainty principle states that certain pairs of properties of quantum particles cannot be simultaneously measured with perfect accuracy. The more precisely you know one property, the less precisely you can know its complementary property. This isn't a limitation of our measuring instruments—it's a fundamental feature of quantum reality.

For quantum computing, the uncertainty principle creates both opportunities and challenges. It contributes to the probabilistic nature of quantum computation, making it impossible to predict exactly what result a quantum computer will produce. However, it also enables quantum computers to process information in ways that classical computers cannot, accessing computational pathways that are fundamentally unavailable to deterministic classical systems.

Quantum Decoherence

Perhaps the greatest challenge in building practical quantum computers stems from quantum decoherence—the process by which quantum systems lose their quantum properties when they interact with their environment. In the classical world, isolation is relatively easy to achieve. You can build a classical computer that operates reliably in various environments, from arctic research stations to desert military bases.

Quantum computers are far more delicate. The quantum states that give these machines their computational power are extraordinarily fragile. Heat, electromagnetic radiation, vibrations, and even cosmic rays can disrupt quantum calculations. Current quantum computers require near-absolute zero temperatures and extensive shielding to maintain quantum coherence for even brief periods.

This fragility explains why quantum computers currently exist primarily in specialized research facilities and cloud computing centers rather than on desktop computers. Overcoming decoherence represents one of the primary engineering challenges in scaling quantum computers to practical applications.

From Bits to Qubits: A Revolutionary Transition

The transition from classical bits to quantum qubits represents more than just a technological upgrade—it's a fundamental reimagining of how information can be stored, processed, and manipulated. Understanding this transition requires examining both what classical bits can and cannot do, and how qubits transcend these limitations.

Classical Bits: The Foundation of Digital Life

Classical computers represent information using bits, each of which stores a single binary digit: either 0 or 1. These bits correspond to physical states in computer hardware—typically, the presence or absence of electrical charge in memory circuits, or the orientation of magnetic fields in storage devices. The reliability and predictability of these physical states have enabled the digital revolution that surrounds us.

Every piece of digital information in your life—from the text in this book to the videos you stream online—ultimately reduces to sequences of 0s and 1s. Computer processors manipulate these bits using logic gates, simple operations that take one or more input bits and produce output bits according to predetermined rules. The NOT gate flips a bit from 0 to 1 or vice versa, while the AND gate outputs 1 only when both of its input bits are 1.

The power of classical computing emerges from combining these simple operations into complex algorithms that can solve sophisticated problems. However, classical bits impose fundamental constraints on how information can be processed. Each bit must be in a definite state at any given time, and processing information requires manipulating these definite states through deterministic operations.

Quantum Bits: Embracing Uncertainty

Qubits operate according to entirely different rules. While a classical bit must be either 0 or 1, a qubit can exist in a superposition of both states simultaneously. This isn't just a more flexible way of storing information—it's a fundamentally different relationship between physical systems and the information they contain.

The state of a qubit can be visualized using a concept called the Bloch sphere, a three-dimensional representation where the north and south poles represent the classical 0 and 1 states, respectively. Any point on the surface of this sphere represents a valid qubit state. States at the north and south poles behave like classical bits, but states elsewhere on the sphere represent genuine superpositions—quantum states that are simultaneously 0 and 1 in measurable, physical ways.

When quantum computers process information, they manipulate these superposition states using quantum gates—operations that rotate qubits around the Bloch sphere. Unlike classical logic gates, all quantum gates are reversible, meaning you can always undo a quantum operation if needed. This reversibility reflects a fundamental symmetry in quantum mechanics and enables quantum computers to perform certain calculations more efficiently than classical systems.

Exponential Information Scaling

The true power of qubits emerges when multiple quantum bits work together. While two classical bits can represent one of four possible states (00, 01, 10, 11), two qubits can exist in a superposition of all four states simultaneously. This parallel processing capability scales exponentially: three qubits can process information equivalent to eight classical bits simultaneously, four qubits equivalent to sixteen classical bits, and so forth.

This exponential scaling explains why quantum computers promise to solve certain problems exponentially faster than classical computers. A quantum computer with just 300 qubits could, in principle, process more information simultaneously than there are atoms in the observable universe. While practical quantum computers face numerous limitations that prevent them from achieving this theoretical maximum, the potential for exponential speedup drives the intense research and investment in quantum technology worldwide.

The Measurement Paradox

The transition from qubits to practical results introduces one of quantum computing's most fascinating challenges. While qubits can exist in superposition states during computation, extracting information from a quantum computer requires measurement, which forces qubits to "choose" definite 0 or 1 states. This measurement process is probabilistic—you can't predict exactly which state a qubit will choose, only the probability of each outcome.

This creates a fundamental paradox in quantum computation. The superposition states that give quantum computers their power are also extremely fragile. Measuring a qubit destroys its superposition, collapsing it into a classical state. Quantum algorithms must therefore be designed carefully to preserve quantum superposition throughout the calculation while still extracting useful information through final measurements.

Successful quantum algorithms solve this paradox through ingenious design. They manipulate quantum states so that correct answers have high probability of being measured, while incorrect answers have low probability. The algorithm might run multiple times to build confidence in the results, but each individual run completes much faster than any classical algorithm could solve the same problem.

Real-World Quantum Advantages

Understanding quantum computing's theoretical advantages is one thing; seeing how these advantages translate into practical applications is another. Several problems demonstrate quantum computing's potential to revolutionize fields from chemistry to cryptography.

Molecular Simulation and Drug Discovery

Classical computers struggle to model molecular systems because molecules are fundamentally quantum mechanical entities. When scientists try to predict how a new drug molecule will interact with proteins in the human body, they're essentially trying to use classical physics to model quantum systems—a task that becomes exponentially difficult as molecules grow larger.

Quantum computers offer a more natural approach to molecular modeling. Since both the quantum computer and the molecules being studied operate according to quantum mechanical principles, quantum computers can simulate molecular behavior more directly and efficiently. This capability could accelerate drug discovery, enabling researchers to test thousands of potential medications virtually before synthesizing and testing them in laboratories.

The pharmaceutical industry currently spends billions of dollars and decades developing new drugs, with most candidates failing during expensive clinical trials. Quantum-powered molecular simulation could identify promising drug candidates much earlier in the development process, potentially reducing both the time and cost required to bring new treatments to patients.

Optimization and Machine Learning

Many real-world problems involve finding the best solution among an enormous number of possibilities. Portfolio managers want to find the optimal allocation of investments across thousands of securities. Logistics companies need to find the most efficient routes for delivery vehicles visiting hundreds of locations. Airlines must schedule crews, gates, and aircraft to minimize delays and costs while satisfying complex regulatory and operational constraints.

These optimization problems often involve evaluating exponentially large numbers of possible solutions. Classical computers approach these problems through various approximation techniques, but they cannot evaluate all possibilities within reasonable timeframes. Quantum computers could explore these vast solution spaces more efficiently, potentially finding better solutions to optimization problems that affect everything from financial markets to supply chain management.

Machine learning represents another area where quantum computers may provide significant advantages. Training artificial intelligence systems requires processing enormous datasets and optimizing complex mathematical functions. Quantum computers could accelerate both the training process and the application of machine learning models, potentially enabling AI systems that are more powerful and efficient than anything possible with classical computers.

Cryptography and Security

The most immediate and concerning application of quantum computing involves breaking current cryptographic systems. In 1994, mathematician Peter Shor developed a quantum algorithm that can factor large numbers exponentially faster than any known classical algorithm. Shor's algorithm poses a direct threat to RSA encryption, the security protocol that protects most internet communications, online banking, and digital commerce.

While large-scale quantum computers capable of running Shor's algorithm don't exist yet, their eventual development will render current encryption methods obsolete. This prospect has prompted governments and corporations worldwide to develop new cryptographic methods that remain secure even against quantum attacks. The race to deploy quantum-resistant security measures represents one of the most urgent practical challenges in preparing for the quantum age.

The Engineering Reality

Despite their theoretical power, building practical quantum computers presents extraordinary engineering challenges that highlight the gap between quantum computing's potential and its current reality. These challenges explain why quantum computers haven't already revolutionized every aspect of computing and why the transition to quantum technology will be gradual rather than sudden.

The Fragility Problem

Quantum computers are extraordinarily sensitive to their environment. The quantum states that enable superposition and entanglement are easily disrupted by heat, electromagnetic radiation, vibrations, and other environmental factors. Current quantum computers operate at temperatures within a few millidegrees of absolute zero—colder than outer space—and require extensive shielding from electromagnetic interference.

This environmental sensitivity means that quantum computers are currently large, expensive machines that require specialized facilities and expert operators. While classical computers evolved from room-sized machines to pocket-sized devices over several decades, quantum computers may always require substantial supporting infrastructure due to the fundamental physics involved.

Error Rates and Quantum Error Correction

Current quantum computers are "noisy," meaning they produce errors at rates that would be unacceptable for classical computers. While classical computers experience error rates of approximately one error per trillion operations, current quantum computers experience errors in roughly one out of every thousand operations. These high error rates limit the complexity and duration of quantum calculations that current systems can perform reliably.

Quantum error correction—the process of detecting and correcting errors in quantum calculations—requires substantial overhead. Current estimates suggest that building a single "logical" qubit that can perform error-free calculations may require hundreds or thousands of physical qubits. This overhead means that practical quantum computers may need millions of physical qubits to perform calculations that would benefit from just hundreds of logical qubits.

Limited Algorithms and Applications

While quantum computers promise exponential speedups for certain problems, they don't provide advantages for all computational tasks. In fact, for many everyday computing applications—word processing, web browsing, playing videos—quantum computers offer no benefits over classical systems and would likely perform worse due to their complexity and error rates.

The number of quantum algorithms that provide clear advantages over classical approaches remains relatively small. Shor's factoring algorithm and Grover's search algorithm represent the most well-known examples, but developing new quantum algorithms requires deep expertise in both quantum mechanics and computer science. The limited library of quantum algorithms constrains the current applications for quantum computers.

Bridging Two Worlds

Quantum computing represents a bridge between the abstract world of quantum mechanics and the practical demands of information processing. This bridge involves translating physical quantum phenomena into computational resources, engineering quantum systems that can maintain coherence long enough to perform useful calculations, and developing algorithms that leverage quantum advantages while managing quantum limitations.

From Physics to Information

The journey from quantum mechanics to quantum computing required recognizing that information itself has physical properties. In classical computing, the distinction between hardware and software is relatively clear—software represents abstract logical operations that can run on various hardware platforms. Quantum computing blurs this distinction because quantum information is intimately connected to the physical properties of quantum systems.

Quantum algorithms must account for the specific physical properties of the quantum hardware they run on. Different types of quantum computers—those based on superconducting circuits, trapped ions, or photonic systems—have different capabilities and limitations that affect algorithm design. This intimate connection between physics and computation means that advancing quantum computing requires simultaneous progress in quantum physics, engineering, and computer science.

The Classical-Quantum Interface

Practical quantum computers don't operate in isolation—they must interface with classical computers that control quantum operations, process measurement results, and manage quantum programs. This classical-quantum interface introduces additional complexity, as classical control systems must coordinate quantum operations with nanosecond precision while processing measurement results that are inherently probabilistic.

The development of software tools for programming quantum computers represents a crucial area of ongoing research. Quantum programming languages must abstract away some of the complexity of quantum mechanics while still giving programmers access to quantum computational advantages. These tools must also handle the translation between classical program descriptions and the precise physical operations required to manipulate quantum states.

Looking Ahead

The strange world of quantum computing represents both an extraordinary opportunity and a significant challenge for our technology-dependent society. Quantum computers promise to solve problems that are fundamentally intractable for classical systems, potentially leading to breakthroughs in medicine, energy, artificial intelligence, and our basic understanding of the universe.

However, realizing this promise requires overcoming substantial engineering challenges and developing new approaches to algorithm design, error correction, and quantum-classical system integration. The timeline for practical quantum computing applications varies dramatically depending on the specific problem and the level of quantum advantage required.

Understanding quantum computing's current capabilities and limitations is essential for making informed decisions about technology investments, security preparations, and career planning in our increasingly digital world. As we'll explore in subsequent chapters, the quantum revolution is not a distant possibility—it's an ongoing transformation that's already beginning to affect industries, governments, and individuals worldwide.

The next chapter will examine how we arrived at this quantum moment, tracing the remarkable history of ideas and innovations that transformed quantum mechanics from an abstract theory about atomic behavior into the foundation for revolutionary computing technology. This historical perspective will illuminate both the scientific breakthroughs and the persistent challenges that continue to shape quantum computing's development.

The quantum puzzle that opens this book—how something can be in multiple states simultaneously—is just the beginning of our journey into a technology that challenges our most basic assumptions about reality while promising to transform our world in ways we're only beginning to imagine.

Chapter 2: The Pioneers - A History of Quantum Computing

The story of quantum computing begins not with engineers tinkering in Silicon Valley garages, but with physicists grappling with some of the most profound mysteries of the universe. Unlike the development of classical computers, which emerged from practical needs during World War II, quantum computing arose from humanity's quest to understand the fundamental nature of reality itself. The journey from abstract theoretical physics to revolutionary computing technology spans more than a century, involving some of the most brilliant minds in scientific history.

This transformation didn't happen overnight. The path from Max Planck's discovery of quantum theory in 1900 to today's quantum computers represents one of the most remarkable intellectual odysseys in human history. Each breakthrough built upon previous discoveries, gradually revealing how the strange properties of quantum mechanics could be harnessed for information processing. The scientists who made these discoveries often had no idea they were laying the groundwork for a computational revolution that would challenge our understanding of what computers can accomplish.

Early Theoretical Foundations

The Quantum Revolution Begins

The foundation of quantum computing traces back to December 14, 1900, when Max Planck presented his solution to the blackbody radiation problem to the German Physical Society. Planck discovered that energy could only be emitted and absorbed in discrete packets, which he called "quanta". This seemingly simple observation shattered the classical view of physics, where energy was thought to be continuous and infinitely divisible.

Planck's discovery revealed that nature operates according to fundamentally different rules at microscopic scales. Energy comes in indivisible chunks, just as matter comes in discrete atoms. This quantization of energy provided the first hint that the microscopic world might operate according to principles that could eventually be exploited for computation. Though Planck himself couldn't have imagined it, his quantum theory contained the seeds of a computational revolution that would unfold over the next century.

The implications of Planck's work extended far beyond solving an obscure physics problem. His quantum hypothesis suggested that the classical physics that governed everyday experience might not apply at atomic scales. This realization opened the door to a new understanding of reality—one where particles could exist in multiple states simultaneously, where observation affected physical outcomes, and where distant particles could be mysteriously connected.

Bohr's Quantum Architecture

Thirteen years after Planck's breakthrough, Niels Bohr revolutionized our understanding of atomic structure with his quantum model of the atom. Previous models had suggested that electrons orbited atomic nuclei like planets around the sun, gradually losing energy and spiraling inward until atoms collapsed. This classical picture couldn't explain why atoms remained stable or why they emitted light at specific wavelengths.

Bohr proposed that electrons could only exist in specific, quantized orbital energy levels around atomic nuclei. Electrons could jump between these levels by absorbing or emitting photons with precise energies, but they couldn't exist in the spaces between these allowed orbits. This model explained atomic stability and the discrete spectral lines observed in atomic emission, providing crucial evidence that quantum effects were real and measurable.

Bohr's quantum atom introduced the concept of discrete quantum states—the idea that quantum systems could only exist in specific, well-defined configurations. This concept would later become central to quantum computing, where qubits exist in discrete quantum states that can be manipulated to perform calculations. The notion that quantum systems have discrete, stable states provided the theoretical foundation for storing and processing quantum information.

The Bohr model also revealed the peculiar relationship between observation and quantum reality. Electrons existed in definite energy levels, but their exact positions and velocities remained fundamentally uncertain. This observation-dependent nature of quantum systems would later become crucial for understanding how quantum computers extract useful information from quantum calculations through measurement.

The Mathematical Revolution

The theoretical foundations of quantum computing crystallized during the mid-1920s when Werner Heisenberg and Erwin Schrödinger independently developed mathematical frameworks for describing quantum phenomena. Heisenberg's matrix mechanics and Schrödinger's wave mechanics provided powerful tools for calculating quantum system behavior, even though they described a reality that seemed to defy common sense.

These mathematical frameworks revealed the full strangeness of quantum mechanics. Particles could exist in superposition states—combinations of multiple classical states that somehow existed simultaneously. The act of measurement caused these superposition states to "collapse" into definite classical outcomes, but before measurement, quantum systems existed in probabilistic combinations of all possible states.

The mathematical structure of quantum mechanics also revealed the phenomenon of entanglement—the ability of quantum particles to become correlated in ways that classical physics couldn't explain. When particles become entangled, measuring one particle instantly affects the state of its entangled partners, regardless of the distance between them. Einstein famously dismissed this "spooky action at a distance" as evidence that quantum mechanics was incomplete, but subsequent experiments confirmed that entanglement is a real physical phenomenon.

These mathematical tools provided the language needed to describe and predict quantum behavior, but they also raised profound questions about the nature of reality itself. The mathematics suggested that quantum systems could exist in multiple states simultaneously and that observation played a fundamental role in determining physical outcomes. These insights would later become essential for understanding how quantum computers process information.

Key Breakthrough Moments

Feynman's Visionary Proposal

The direct intellectual lineage of quantum computing begins with Richard Feynman's prescient observation in 1981. Speaking at a conference on the physics of computation, Feynman posed a deceptively simple question: if nature operates quantum mechanically, why shouldn't we build computers that operate quantum mechanically too? His insight was that classical computers would always struggle to simulate quantum systems because they were fundamentally trying to use classical physics to model quantum phenomena.

Feynman recognized that quantum systems contain exponentially more information than classical systems of comparable size. A classical computer attempting to simulate a quantum system must track all possible quantum states and their interactions, leading to computational requirements that grow exponentially with system size. Even modest quantum systems quickly overwhelm the most powerful classical computers.

But Feynman's breakthrough insight was that quantum computers could potentially simulate quantum systems naturally and efficiently. Since both the computer and the system being simulated would operate according to quantum mechanical principles, the simulation wouldn't require the exponential overhead that classical computers face. This vision of quantum simulation became one of the most compelling early applications for quantum computing and remains a major driver of quantum research today.

Feynman's proposal also introduced the concept that computation itself might be a physical process governed by the laws of physics. Rather than viewing computers as abstract information processors that could be implemented on any physical platform, Feynman suggested that the physical properties of computational systems fundamentally constrained their capabilities. This physics-first approach to computation opened entirely new avenues for thinking about what computers could accomplish.

The Universal Quantum Computer

David Deutsch, working at Oxford University in the 1980s, transformed Feynman's vision into a concrete theoretical framework. Deutsch is often called the "father of quantum computing" because he provided the first rigorous description of a universal quantum computer—a machine that could efficiently simulate any physical process that occurs in nature.

Deutsch's work built upon Alan Turing's earlier concept of universal classical computation, which showed that any computation that could be performed by one classical computer could, in principle, be performed by any other classical computer given sufficient time and memory. Deutsch extended this universality principle to quantum systems, showing that a sufficiently powerful quantum computer could simulate any quantum system efficiently.

This universality principle had profound implications. If quantum computers could efficiently simulate any quantum system, they could potentially solve problems involving molecular chemistry, materials science, and fundamental physics that remained intractable for classical computers. Deutsch's theoretical framework provided the foundation for quantum algorithm development and established quantum computing as a legitimate field of computer science research.

Deutsch also developed the first quantum algorithm, known as the Deutsch algorithm, which demonstrated that quantum computers could solve certain problems faster than classical computers. Though the problem his algorithm solved was relatively artificial, it provided the first concrete proof that quantum computers could offer genuine computational advantages over classical systems.

Shor's Algorithm: The Cryptographic Earthquake

The development that truly captured worldwide attention came in 1994 when Peter Shor, working at Bell Labs, developed a quantum algorithm for factoring large integers. Shor's algorithm demonstrated that a sufficiently powerful quantum computer could factor numbers exponentially faster than any known classical algorithm. This breakthrough had immediate and dramatic implications for cybersecurity, since most modern encryption systems rely on the assumption that factoring large numbers is computationally intractable.

Shor's algorithm works by transforming the factoring problem into a period-finding problem, which quantum computers can solve efficiently using quantum Fourier transforms. The algorithm doesn't directly factor numbers; instead, it finds patterns in the mathematical structure of multiplication that reveal the factors of composite numbers. This indirect approach exemplifies the clever mathematical insights required to design effective quantum algorithms.

The announcement of Shor's algorithm sent shockwaves through the cryptographic community and government security agencies worldwide. If large-scale quantum computers could be built, they would render most current encryption methods obsolete overnight. This prospect spurred massive investments in both quantum computer development and the creation of new cryptographic methods that would remain secure against quantum attacks.

Shor's work also demonstrated the potential economic impact of quantum computing. The global digital economy depends on cryptographic security for everything from online banking to secure communications. A technology that could break these security systems represented both an enormous threat to existing infrastructure and a tremendous opportunity for those who could harness quantum computing's power responsibly.

Grover's Search Revolution

Two years after Shor's breakthrough, Lov Grover at Bell Labs developed another fundamental quantum algorithm that demonstrated quantum computing's potential beyond cryptography. Grover's algorithm addresses the problem of searching through unsorted databases—a ubiquitous challenge in computer science that affects everything from internet search engines to artificial intelligence systems.

Classical computers searching through an unsorted database of N items must, in the worst case, examine every item before finding the target, requiring N operations on average. Grover's algorithm accomplishes the same task in roughly N*N* operations, providing a quadratic speedup that might seem modest compared to Shor's exponential advantage but applies to a much broader range of problems.

The beauty of Grover's algorithm lies in its generality. Unlike Shor's algorithm, which applies specifically to factoring and related mathematical problems, Grover's algorithm can accelerate any unstructured search problem. This includes optimization problems, machine learning applications, and database queries that form the backbone of modern computing systems.

Grover's work also revealed important theoretical limits on quantum computing. While quantum computers can provide dramatic speedups for some problems, they cannot solve all problems exponentially faster than classical computers. Grover's quadratic speedup for search problems appears to be optimal—no quantum algorithm can do better. This limitation helped establish realistic expectations for quantum computing's capabilities.

The Visionaries Who Made It Possible

Richard Feynman: The Quantum Prophet

Richard Feynman stands as perhaps the most influential figure in quantum computing's prehistory, though he never built a quantum computer himself. His contributions to quantum electrodynamics and his deep understanding of quantum mechanics positioned him uniquely to envision how quantum properties could be harnessed for computation.

Feynman's approach to physics emphasized physical intuition over mathematical formalism. He had an extraordinary ability to visualize quantum phenomena and explain complex physics concepts through simple analogies and thought experiments. This intuitive approach led him to recognize that the exponential complexity of quantum systems, which made them difficult to simulate classically, could become a computational resource if properly harnessed.

Beyond his specific technical contributions, Feynman embodied the interdisciplinary thinking essential for quantum computing development. He moved fluidly between theoretical physics, experimental investigation, and practical applications. His famous lectures on computation demonstrated how physical principles constrain computational possibilities, establishing the intellectual framework that would guide quantum computing research for decades.

Feynman's influence extended beyond his technical contributions. His infectious enthusiasm for discovery and his willingness to challenge conventional thinking inspired generations of researchers to explore the boundaries between physics and computation. Many quantum computing pioneers cite Feynman's vision as the initial inspiration for their careers in quantum research.

David Deutsch: The Theoretical Architect

If Feynman provided the inspiration for quantum computing, David Deutsch supplied the theoretical architecture. Working at Oxford University during the 1980s, Deutsch developed the mathematical foundations that transformed quantum computing from an intriguing possibility into a rigorous field of computer science research.

Deutsch's most significant contribution was proving that quantum computers could be universal—capable of efficiently simulating any physical process that occurs in nature. This universality principle extended Alan Turing's work on classical computation into the quantum realm, showing that quantum computers weren't just specialized devices for solving particular problems, but potentially universal computational tools.

Deutsch also developed the first quantum algorithm, demonstrating that quantum computers could solve certain problems faster than classical computers. Though his algorithm addressed a relatively artificial problem, it provided the first concrete proof that quantum computation could offer genuine advantages over classical approaches. This proof-of-concept opened the door for more practical quantum algorithms that would follow.

Perhaps equally important, Deutsch helped establish the theoretical framework for quantum algorithm design. He showed how quantum algorithms could leverage interference effects to amplify correct answers while canceling out incorrect ones. This insight became a template for designing more sophisticated quantum algorithms that could tackle real-world problems.

Peter Shor: The Cryptographic Revolutionary

Peter Shor's development of his famous factoring algorithm represents one of the most consequential breakthroughs in computer science history. Working at Bell Labs in the early 1990s, Shor recognized that the mathematical structure of factoring problems could be transformed into period-finding problems that quantum computers could solve efficiently.

Shor's algorithm demonstrated that quantum computers weren't just theoretical curiosities—they could solve problems with immediate practical importance. The ability to factor large numbers efficiently threatened the security foundations of the digital economy, making quantum computing an urgent concern for governments and corporations worldwide.

The development of Shor's algorithm also showcased the sophisticated mathematical insights required for quantum algorithm design. Shor combined number theory, classical algorithms, and quantum mechanical principles in novel ways, creating an algorithm that was both mathematically elegant and practically devastating for current cryptographic systems.

Beyond its immediate impact on cryptography, Shor's work established a template for quantum algorithm development that influenced subsequent research. His approach of identifying classical problems with hidden mathematical structure that quantum computers could exploit became a standard strategy for developing new quantum algorithms.

The First Experimental Demonstrations

The transition from theoretical quantum computing to experimental reality began in the late 1990s with modest but crucial demonstrations. In 1998, researchers at Oxford University and IBM's Almaden Research Center independently demonstrated the first experimental implementations of quantum algorithms. Using nuclear magnetic resonance (NMR) techniques, they built simple 2-qubit quantum computers that could solve artificial problems designed to showcase quantum computational advantages.

These early experiments faced significant skepticism from the quantum computing community. The NMR systems used billions of molecules as qubits, and critics argued that the quantum states in these systems were too "mixed" to provide genuine quantum advantages. The experiments demonstrated quantum algorithms working in principle, but whether they actually outperformed classical computers remained controversial.

Despite these limitations, the early NMR experiments proved that quantum algorithms could be implemented on real physical systems. Researchers successfully demonstrated Deutsch's algorithm, Grover's search algorithm, and even a simplified version of Shor's factoring algorithm. These proof-of-concept experiments validated the theoretical foundations of quantum computing and provided valuable experience in the practical challenges of building quantum systems.

The experimental work also revealed the extraordinary difficulty of maintaining quantum coherence in real physical systems. The delicate quantum states required for computation lasted only microseconds before environmental interference destroyed them. This discovery highlighted the enormous engineering challenges that would need to be overcome before quantum computers could solve practical problems.

The Commercial Awakening

D-Wave's Bold Gamble

The transition from academic research to commercial development began in earnest with D-Wave Systems' announcement in 2007 that they had built the world's first commercial quantum computer. D-Wave's approach differed significantly from the gate-based quantum computers envisioned by academic researchers. Instead, they developed quantum annealing systems designed to solve optimization problems by finding the lowest energy states of quantum systems.

D-Wave's 16-qubit system generated enormous controversy within the quantum computing community. Critics argued that the company's quantum annealing approach didn't provide the full power of universal quantum computation and questioned whether their systems offered genuine quantum advantages over classical computers. The debate highlighted fundamental questions about what constitutes "true" quantum computing and how to measure quantum computational advantages.

Despite the controversy, D-Wave's commercial approach attracted significant attention from investors and potential customers. The company demonstrated that quantum computing could transition from academic research to commercial development, even if the technology wasn't yet mature enough to solve practical problems more efficiently than classical computers.

D-Wave's persistence through years of skepticism ultimately vindicated their approach. In 2011, they released the D-Wave One, a 128-qubit quantum annealer that marked the first commercial quantum computer available for purchase. While debates about D-Wave's quantum advantages continued, their systems provided valuable platforms for researchers to explore quantum algorithms and applications.

IBM's Quantum Cloud Revolution

The democratization of quantum computing accelerated dramatically in 2016 when IBM launched the IBM Quantum Experience, making quantum computing accessible through cloud-based platforms. For the first time, anyone with an internet connection could run quantum algorithms on real quantum hardware. This breakthrough transformed quantum computing from an exclusive research domain into a technology that students, researchers, and developers worldwide could explore directly.

IBM's 5-qubit quantum processor, accessible through their cloud platform, might seem modest compared to today's systems, but it represented a fundamental shift in quantum computing accessibility. The platform included educational resources, algorithm tutorials, and development tools that allowed users to learn quantum programming without requiring expensive quantum hardware or specialized laboratory facilities.

The cloud-based approach also demonstrated quantum computing's potential for distributed access. Unlike classical computers, which require physical possession of hardware, quantum computers could be shared among multiple users through cloud interfaces. This sharing model made economic sense given the high costs and specialized infrastructure required for quantum systems.

IBM's quantum cloud sparked a global community of quantum programmers and researchers. Universities began incorporating quantum computing into their curricula, startups explored quantum applications, and major corporations started investigating how quantum computers might eventually impact their industries. The platform provided crucial feedback on quantum programming tools and algorithms, accelerating the development of quantum software ecosystems.

The Scientific Method in Action

Building on Failures

The history of quantum computing illustrates the scientific method in action, showing how apparent failures and limitations often lead to crucial breakthroughs. Early quantum computers couldn't maintain coherence for more than microseconds, leading some critics to dismiss quantum computing as fundamentally impractical. However, these limitations spurred research into quantum error correction, decoherence suppression, and more robust quantum architectures.

The controversy surrounding D-Wave's early systems exemplifies how scientific debate advances understanding. Critics who questioned D-Wave's quantum advantages weren't merely being negative—they were applying rigorous standards for quantum computational advantages that pushed the field toward more rigorous experimental validation. This scientific scrutiny ultimately strengthened quantum computing by forcing researchers to develop better metrics for quantum performance and more convincing demonstrations of quantum advantages.

The apparent setbacks in early quantum computing research often revealed important insights about the nature of quantum computation itself. When researchers discovered that early NMR quantum computers contained no entanglement, this finding led to deeper investigations into the quantum resources required for computational speedup. These investigations expanded our understanding of quantum computation and guided the development of more powerful quantum systems.

The First Quantum Algorithms in Action

The year 1998 marked a watershed moment in quantum computing history with the first experimental demonstrations of quantum algorithms. Research teams at Oxford University and IBM's Almaden Research Center independently implemented quantum algorithms on physical quantum systems, transforming abstract mathematical concepts into working computational demonstrations.

These pioneering experiments used nuclear magnetic resonance (NMR) techniques to create 2-qubit quantum computers capable of solving Deutsch's algorithm—a simple problem designed to showcase quantum computational advantages. The systems used billions of molecules as qubits, with each molecule's nuclear spins representing quantum information. While primitive by today's standards, these experiments proved that quantum algorithms could run on real physical systems rather than existing only in theoretical frameworks.

The same year witnessed the first experimental implementation of Grover's search algorithm, demonstrating that quantum computers could accelerate search problems beyond the capabilities of classical systems. These early demonstrations provided concrete evidence that quantum computing represented more than just mathematical curiosities—they could solve actual computational problems using measurably different approaches than classical computers.

However, controversy surrounded these early experiments. Critics argued that the NMR systems used were too "noisy" and contained no genuine entanglement—the quantum correlation that many researchers considered essential for quantum computational advantages. This debate sparked important investigations into the quantum resources required for computational speedup and helped establish more rigorous criteria for evaluating quantum computing claims.

The Engineering Breakthrough

While theorists developed quantum algorithms and experimentalists demonstrated quantum computation principles, engineers worked on the practical challenges of building scalable quantum systems. The late 1990s brought crucial developments in quantum error correction, showing how quantum computers could overcome the inherent fragility of quantum information.

Peter Shor's development of quantum error-correcting codes in 1995 addressed one of quantum computing's most fundamental challenges. Quantum states are extraordinarily fragile, losing their quantum properties through interaction with the environment—a process called decoherence. Shor's error correction schemes showed how multiple physical qubits could be combined to create more robust "logical" qubits that could maintain quantum information even when individual physical qubits experienced errors.

David DiVincenzo at IBM articulated practical criteria for building useful quantum computers, establishing benchmarks that guided engineering efforts. His five conditions for quantum computing included scalable physical qubits, reliable qubit initialization, long quantum coherence times, accurate quantum operations, and efficient quantum measurement. These criteria provided roadmaps for quantum hardware development and helped focus research efforts on the most critical technical challenges.

The development of superconducting qubits represented another crucial engineering breakthrough. In 1999, researchers demonstrated that superconducting circuits could function as qubits, operating at temperatures near absolute zero where electrical resistance disappears. These solid-state qubits offered advantages in terms of fabrication using semiconductor manufacturing techniques and integration with classical electronics.

The Modern Era Begins

The Quantum Annealing Revolution

D-Wave Systems' announcement of the D-Wave One in 2011 marked the beginning of commercial quantum computing. The 128-qubit quantum annealer represented the first quantum computer available for purchase, transforming quantum computing from an academic pursuit into a commercial technology. While D-Wave's approach differed from universal gate-based quantum computers, their success demonstrated that quantum effects could be harnessed for practical computational applications.

The D-Wave One used quantum annealing to solve optimization problems—a specialized form of quantum computation that finds minimum energy configurations of quantum systems. This approach proved particularly suitable for problems involving scheduling, logistics, and resource allocation, attracting customers from industries ranging from financial services to aerospace engineering.

D-Wave's commercial success validated the economic potential of quantum computing while highlighting the diversity of quantum computational approaches. The company's focus on specific application domains showed that quantum computers didn't need to be universal to provide value, encouraging other companies to develop specialized quantum systems for particular problem classes.

The quantum annealing approach also demonstrated the importance of matching quantum hardware capabilities to algorithmic requirements. Rather than attempting to build universal quantum computers immediately, D-Wave focused on quantum systems optimized for specific types of problems. This application-driven approach influenced subsequent quantum computing development strategies across the industry.

The Cloud Computing Democracy

IBM's launch of the IBM Quantum Experience in 2016 democratized access to quantum computing technology. The cloud-based platform provided free access to a 5-qubit quantum processor, enabling anyone with internet access to run quantum algorithms on real quantum hardware. This accessibility transformed quantum computing from an exclusive research domain into a technology that students, educators, and developers worldwide could explore directly.

The platform included comprehensive educational resources, quantum algorithm tutorials, and development tools that lowered barriers to quantum programming. Users could design quantum circuits using intuitive graphical interfaces, run algorithms on actual quantum processors, and compare results with classical simulations. This hands-on experience proved invaluable for building the quantum computing workforce and expanding the community of quantum researchers.

IBM's cloud approach also demonstrated quantum computing's potential for distributed access models. Unlike classical computers, which typically require physical ownership of hardware, quantum computers could be shared efficiently among multiple users through cloud interfaces. This sharing model made economic sense given the high costs and specialized infrastructure requirements of quantum systems.

The success of IBM's quantum cloud platform sparked similar offerings from other companies. Amazon launched Braket, providing access to quantum computers from multiple vendors through a single cloud interface. Google, Microsoft, and other tech giants developed their own quantum cloud services, creating a competitive ecosystem that accelerated quantum computing adoption and development.

The history of quantum computing reveals a remarkable transformation from abstract theoretical physics to practical computing technology. The journey required contributions from physicists who uncovered quantum mechanics' fundamental principles, mathematicians who developed quantum algorithms, and engineers who built the first working quantum systems. Each breakthrough built upon previous discoveries, gradually revealing how quantum mechanics' strange properties could be harnessed for revolutionary computational capabilities.

This historical perspective illuminates both the scientific achievements that made quantum computing possible and the persistent challenges that continue to shape the field's development. The transition from Planck's quantum theory to today's quantum cloud platforms demonstrates humanity's ability to transform fundamental scientific discoveries into transformative technologies, even when those discoveries initially seem to defy common sense and practical application.

Chapter 3: The Building Blocks - How Quantum Computers Work

Understanding how quantum computers work requires entering a realm where the familiar rules of everyday physics no longer apply. In this strange quantum world, objects can exist in multiple states simultaneously, distant particles can instantly affect each other, and the very act of observation changes physical reality. These aren't just abstract theoretical concepts—they're the operational principles that quantum computers harness to solve problems that would overwhelm classical systems.

The challenge of explaining quantum computing lies in bridging the gap between quantum mechanical phenomena that seem to violate common sense and practical computing applications that solve real-world problems. We must understand not just what quantum computers can do, but how they accomplish these seemingly impossible feats through the careful manipulation of quantum mechanical properties.

Building this understanding requires examining three fundamental components of quantum computation: the quantum mechanical phenomena that provide computational resources, the quantum gates and circuits that manipulate quantum information, and the error correction methods that protect quantum calculations from environmental interference. Each component presents both extraordinary opportunities and significant engineering challenges that shape quantum computing's current capabilities and future potential.

Superposition and Entanglement Explained

The Reality of Superposition

Superposition represents perhaps the most counterintuitive aspect of quantum mechanics, yet it forms the foundation of quantum computing's computational power. Unlike classical bits that must be definitively 0 or 1, qubits can exist in quantum superposition states that are simultaneously 0 and 1 until measured. This isn't merely a limitation of our knowledge about the qubit's "true" state—superposition represents a genuine physical phenomenon where quantum systems exist in combinations of multiple classical states.

To visualize superposition, imagine a coin spinning in the air. While spinning, the coin isn't definitively heads or tails—it exists in a superposition of both possibilities. However, when the coin lands, it must choose one definite outcome. Qubits behave similarly, existing in superposition states during quantum computations before "collapsing" into definite 0 or 1 states when measured.

The mathematical description of superposition reveals its computational significance. A qubit in superposition can be represented as a combination: $\alpha|0\rangle+\beta|1\rangle\alpha|0\rangle+\beta|1\rangle$, where $\alpha\alpha$ and $\beta\beta$ are complex numbers that determine the probability of measuring 0 or 1 respectively. The notation $|0\rangle|0\rangle$ and $|1\rangle|1\rangle$ represents the quantum states corresponding to classical 0 and 1 bits. The complex coefficients $\alpha\alpha$ and $\beta\beta$ encode much more information than classical bits can contain, providing quantum computers with enhanced information storage capabilities.

When quantum computers process information, they manipulate these superposition coefficients to perform calculations on all possible input states simultaneously. A quantum computer with n qubits can process $2n2n$ classical bit strings at once, enabling parallel exploration of exponentially large solution spaces. This parallel processing capability explains why quantum computers can solve certain problems exponentially faster than classical systems.

Understanding Entanglement's Computational Power

Entanglement extends superposition's power by creating quantum correlations between multiple qubits that cannot be explained by classical physics. When qubits become entangled, measuring one qubit instantly determines properties of its entangled partners, regardless of the physical distance separating them. This instantaneous correlation—which Einstein called "spooky action at a distance"—provides quantum computers with a computational resource that has no classical equivalent.

Entanglement enables qubits to work together in fundamentally new ways. Classical computers process information through local operations—each bit affects only nearby bits through direct physical connections. Entangled qubits can coordinate their behavior without requiring direct physical communication, enabling quantum algorithms to access global information about computational problems more efficiently than classical approaches.

The mathematical structure of entanglement reveals why it's essential for quantum computational advantages. Simple quantum superposition allows parallel processing of multiple input states, but entanglement enables quantum computers to create correlations between different parts of the computation. These correlations allow quantum algorithms to extract global properties of problems that would require exponentially many classical operations to determine.

Creating and maintaining entanglement represents one of quantum computing's greatest technical challenges. Entangled states are even more fragile than simple superposition states, requiring extraordinary isolation from environmental interference. The process of generating entanglement between qubits must be precisely controlled to create the specific quantum correlations needed for particular algorithms.

Quantum Interference and Computation

Quantum computers harness interference effects to amplify correct answers while canceling incorrect ones. Just as sound waves can constructively or destructively interfere to create louder or quieter sounds, quantum states can interfere to increase or decrease the probability of measuring particular outcomes.

Quantum algorithms are designed to create interference patterns that systematically amplify the probability of measuring correct solutions while diminishing the probability of measuring incorrect ones. This selective amplification allows quantum computers to find needles in exponentially large haystacks by making correct answers more likely to appear during measurement.

The design of quantum interference patterns requires sophisticated mathematical analysis. Algorithm designers must understand how different quantum operations affect superposition coefficients and how these coefficients combine during quantum computations. The goal is to orchestrate quantum interference so that many incorrect solution paths cancel each other out while correct solution paths reinforce each other.

This interference-based approach to computation has no classical analog. Classical computers examine solutions sequentially or through parallel processing on separate processors. Quantum computers examine multiple solutions simultaneously and use quantum interference to guide their search toward correct answers. This fundamental difference in computational approach enables quantum speedups that cannot be achieved through classical parallelization alone.

Quantum Gates and Circuits

Single-Qubit Operations

Quantum computation builds from simple operations called quantum gates that manipulate individual qubits or pairs of qubits. Single-qubit gates rotate qubits around the Bloch sphere—a geometric representation where quantum states correspond to points on a sphere's surface. The north and south poles represent classical 0 and 1 states respectively, while other points represent superposition states.

The most fundamental single-qubit gates include the Pauli-X gate (which flips a qubit from 0 to 1 or vice versa), the Pauli-Y gate (which performs a more complex rotation), and the Pauli-Z gate (which flips the phase of a quantum state without changing the probability of measuring 0 or 1). The Hadamard gate creates superposition by rotating qubits from classical 0 or 1 states to equal superposition states, where both outcomes are equally likely when measured.

These single-qubit operations provide the basic building blocks for quantum algorithms, but they cannot create the entanglement necessary for quantum computational advantages. Just as classical computers require operations that affect multiple bits simultaneously, quantum computers need multi-qubit gates to create the quantum correlations that enable exponential speedups.

The precision required for single-qubit operations highlights quantum computing's engineering challenges. Quantum gates must be implemented with extraordinary accuracy—errors in gate operations accumulate quickly and can destroy the delicate quantum states needed for computation. Current quantum computers achieve gate fidelities of approximately 99.9% for single-qubit operations, but even these small error rates limit the complexity of quantum calculations that can be performed reliably.

Two-Qubit Gates and Entanglement Generation

Two-qubit gates enable quantum computers to create entanglement and perform the complex operations necessary for quantum algorithms. The most important two-qubit gate is the controlled-NOT (CNOT) gate, which flips the state of a target qubit based on the state of a control qubit. If the control qubit is in state 1, the target qubit is flipped; if the control qubit is in state 0, the target qubit remains unchanged.

The CNOT gate seems simple, but when applied to qubits in superposition states, it creates entanglement between the control and target qubits. Starting with two independent qubits in superposition and applying a CNOT gate produces an entangled state where the qubits are quantum mechanically correlated. This entanglement generation capability makes the CNOT gate essential for quantum algorithms that require quantum correlations.

Other important two-qubit gates include the controlled-Z gate (which applies a phase flip based on the control qubit's state) and the controlled-rotation gates (which apply arbitrary single-qubit rotations conditionally). These gates provide quantum programmers with the tools needed to create specific entanglement patterns required by different quantum algorithms.

The implementation of two-qubit gates presents significantly greater technical challenges than single-qubit operations. Two-qubit gates require precise control over interactions between qubits, often involving carefully timed pulses of electromagnetic radiation or precisely controlled physical forces. Current quantum computers achieve two-qubit gate fidelities of approximately 99% to 99.9%, with the lower fidelity reflecting the increased complexity of multi-qubit operations.

Quantum Circuit Architecture

Quantum algorithms are implemented using quantum circuits—sequences of quantum gates applied to collections of qubits. Unlike classical circuits, which process information through irreversible logical operations, quantum circuits consist entirely of reversible operations that preserve quantum information throughout the computation.

Quantum circuit design follows principles that differ significantly from classical computer architecture. Classical computers can copy information freely, allowing the same data to be processed by multiple parts of the system simultaneously. Quantum information cannot be copied due to the no-cloning theorem—a fundamental principle of quantum mechanics that prohibits creating perfect copies of unknown quantum states. This limitation requires quantum algorithms to be designed with careful attention to information flow and resource management.

The reversibility of quantum operations also constrains quantum circuit design. Every quantum gate can be "undone" by applying its inverse operation, reflecting the time-reversible nature of quantum mechanical evolution. This reversibility enables quantum computers to explore multiple computational paths and backtrack when necessary, but it also means that quantum algorithms cannot simply discard intermediate results as classical algorithms often do.

Quantum circuits must also account for the probabilistic nature of quantum measurement. The final step in most quantum algorithms involves measuring qubits to extract classical information, but this measurement destroys the quantum superposition states that enabled the computation. Quantum circuit designers must ensure that useful information becomes concentrated in measurable quantum states before the measurement process occurs.

Universal Quantum Computation

A remarkable property of quantum computation is that a small set of quantum gates can implement any possible quantum algorithm—a property called universal quantum computation. Just as classical computers can implement any classical algorithm using combinations of simple logical operations, quantum computers can implement any quantum algorithm using combinations of single-qubit gates and one type of two-qubit gate.

The most commonly used universal gate set consists of all single-qubit rotations plus the CNOT gate. This relatively simple collection of operations can approximate any quantum computation to arbitrary accuracy, providing quantum programmers with the tools needed to implement complex quantum algorithms. The universality of quantum computation means that advances in implementing these basic operations translate directly into improvements in quantum computing capabilities.

However, universal quantum computation doesn't mean that all quantum algorithms are equally easy to implement. Some algorithms require many more gates than others, and the number of gates affects both the computation time and the accumulation of errors. Quantum circuit optimization—finding efficient implementations of quantum algorithms using available gates—represents an active area of research that significantly impacts quantum computing performance.

The universality principle also guides quantum hardware development. Rather than building specialized quantum computers for each application, researchers can focus on building universal quantum computers that can run any quantum algorithm. This approach enables quantum computers to tackle diverse problems and allows software development to proceed independently of specific hardware implementations.

The Challenge of Quantum Error Correction

The Fragility Dilemma

Quantum computers face a fundamental challenge that classical computers largely avoid: the information they process is extraordinarily fragile. Quantum states that enable superposition and entanglement can be destroyed by virtually any interaction with the environment, including heat, electromagnetic radiation, vibrations, and even cosmic rays. This environmental sensitivity means that quantum information degrades continuously during computation, requiring active protection to maintain quantum computational advantages.

The fragility of quantum information stems from the same quantum mechanical principles that provide computational power. Superposition states represent delicate balances between different quantum possibilities, and entanglement creates correlations that depend on precise phase relationships between quantum states. Environmental interference disrupts these delicate balances and correlations, causing quantum computers to lose their quantum properties and behave more like classical systems.

Current quantum computers experience error rates that would be catastrophic for classical systems. While classical computers achieve error rates of approximately one error per trillion operations, quantum computers currently experience errors in roughly one out of every hundred to one thousand operations. These high error rates limit the length and complexity of quantum calculations that current systems can perform reliably.

The time scale of quantum decoherence varies depending on the physical implementation of qubits. Superconducting qubits maintain coherence for microseconds to milliseconds, while trapped ion qubits can maintain coherence for seconds to minutes. These coherence times determine how many quantum operations can be performed before environmental interference destroys the quantum states needed for computation.

Quantum Error Correction Principles

Quantum error correction addresses the fragility problem by using multiple physical qubits to encode each logical qubit of quantum information. Just as classical computers use error-correcting codes to protect data stored on unreliable media, quantum computers can use quantum error-correcting codes to protect quantum information from environmental interference.

However, quantum error correction faces challenges that don't exist in classical computing. The no-cloning theorem prohibits making perfect copies of quantum information, preventing quantum computers from using simple redundancy schemes that work well for classical data. Additionally, measuring quantum states to detect errors destroys the quantum information being protected, requiring more sophisticated approaches to error detection and correction.

Quantum error correction works by encoding logical qubits in entangled states of multiple physical qubits. These encoding schemes are designed so that single-qubit errors affect the encoded quantum information in detectable ways without destroying the logical quantum state. Quantum error correction circuits can detect these error signatures and apply corrective operations to restore the original quantum information.

The most promising quantum error correction approaches require substantial overhead—potentially hundreds or thousands of physical qubits to encode each logical qubit that can perform error-free quantum operations. This overhead represents one of the primary challenges in scaling quantum computers to practical applications, as it multiplies the number of physical qubits needed for useful quantum calculations.

The Surface Code Revolution

Among various quantum error correction schemes, the surface code has emerged as the most promising approach for near-term quantum computers. The surface code arranges qubits in a two-dimensional grid where logical qubits are encoded in the collective state of many physical qubits. Error detection occurs through measurements of specific qubit combinations that reveal whether errors have occurred without destroying the encoded quantum information.

The surface code's appeal lies in its practical implementation requirements. Unlike other quantum error correction schemes that require complex qubit connectivity patterns, the surface code works with nearest-neighbor interactions between qubits arranged in a simple grid. This requirement matches the capabilities of current quantum hardware platforms, making the surface code a practical choice for implementing error correction on existing quantum systems.

The surface code also provides a clear scaling pathway for quantum error correction. Larger surface code patches can correct more errors and provide better protection for logical qubits, but they require more physical qubits and more complex error correction circuits. This scaling relationship allows quantum computer architects to trade physical qubit resources for logical qubit quality, optimizing quantum systems for specific computational requirements.

Recent theoretical and experimental work has demonstrated surface code implementations on small quantum processors, validating the basic principles of this error correction approach. These demonstrations show that quantum error correction can indeed protect quantum information from environmental interference, though current implementations don't yet achieve the error suppression rates needed for practical quantum computing applications.

Fault-Tolerant Quantum Computing

The ultimate goal of quantum error correction is fault-tolerant quantum computing—the ability to perform quantum calculations with arbitrarily low error rates by using sufficiently large numbers of physical qubits. Fault-tolerant quantum computers would overcome the current limitations imposed by quantum decoherence, enabling quantum algorithms to run for extended periods without degradation.

Achieving fault tolerance requires not just error correction, but fault-tolerant implementation of quantum gates and measurements. Every operation in a fault-tolerant quantum computer must be designed to prevent single errors from spreading and corrupting multiple logical qubits. This requirement adds substantial complexity to quantum circuit design and implementation.

The threshold theorem provides theoretical foundation for fault-tolerant quantum computing by proving that quantum error correction can suppress errors indefinitely if the underlying physical error rates remain below specific thresholds. Current estimates suggest that physical qubit error rates must be reduced to approximately 0.01% or lower to enable fault-tolerant quantum computing with reasonable overhead.

Current quantum computers operate in the "noisy intermediate-scale quantum" (NISQ) regime, where error rates are too high for full fault tolerance but low enough to enable limited quantum algorithms. NISQ devices can demonstrate quantum advantages for specific problems while providing platforms for developing and testing quantum error correction techniques. The transition from NISQ devices to fault-tolerant quantum computers represents one of the most significant challenges and opportunities in quantum computing development.

Physical Implementation Challenges

Qubit Technologies and Trade-offs

Different physical platforms for implementing qubits present distinct advantages and challenges that affect quantum computer design and capabilities. Superconducting qubits, based on Josephson junctions operating at millikelvin temperatures, currently dominate commercial quantum computing systems. These qubits can be fabricated using semiconductor manufacturing techniques and integrated with classical electronics, but they require expensive dilution refrigerators to maintain superconducting conditions.

Trapped ion qubits use individual ions confined by electromagnetic fields as quantum information storage and processing elements. These systems offer exceptionally long coherence times and high-fidelity quantum operations, but they typically operate more slowly than superconducting systems and face challenges in scaling to large numbers of qubits. The precise control required for trapped ion systems demands sophisticated laser systems and electromagnetic field generation.

Photonic qubits encode quantum information in individual photons, offering advantages for quantum communication and some types of quantum computation. Photonic systems can operate at room temperature and naturally resist certain types of environmental interference, but they face challenges in creating the strong nonlinear interactions needed for universal quantum computation. Recent advances in photonic quantum computing have demonstrated promising approaches to overcoming these limitations.

Neutral atom quantum computers use individual atoms trapped by optical fields as qubits, combining advantages of trapped ion systems with potentially better scalability. These systems can create flexible qubit connectivity patterns and demonstrate impressive coherence properties, but they require complex optical systems for qubit control and manipulation.

Scaling Challenges

Building quantum computers with hundreds or thousands of qubits requires solving numerous engineering challenges that become more difficult as system size increases. Crosstalk between qubits—unwanted interactions that can corrupt quantum states—becomes more problematic in larger systems where qubits are packed more densely. Control electronics must deliver precisely timed pulses to individual qubits while minimizing interference between control signals.

The classical electronics needed to control quantum computers scale dramatically with the number of qubits. Each qubit requires multiple control lines for initialization, manipulation, and measurement, leading to complex wiring challenges in systems with many qubits. The heat generated by classical electronics must be carefully managed to avoid warming the quantum processor and destroying quantum coherence.

Quantum error correction compounds these scaling challenges by requiring additional overhead for every logical qubit. A quantum computer with 1000 logical qubits might need millions of physical qubits when error correction overhead is included. The classical processing required to perform real-time error correction on such systems would require substantial computational resources, creating feedback loops between quantum and classical system requirements.

The Quantum Advantage Threshold

Current quantum computers exist in a transitional phase where they can demonstrate quantum algorithms but don't yet provide clear practical advantages over classical computers for most problems. This limitation reflects both the current scale of quantum systems and the sophisticated classical algorithms and hardware that have been developed to solve the same problems quantum computers target.

Achieving quantum advantage—solving practical problems faster than classical computers—requires quantum systems that are both large enough and reliable enough to run complex quantum algorithms. The exact requirements vary by application, but estimates suggest that factoring cryptographically relevant numbers would require quantum computers with thousands of logical qubits, potentially requiring millions of physical qubits when error correction is included.

The race to demonstrate quantum advantage has driven rapid improvements in quantum hardware capabilities. Companies and research institutions regularly announce new quantum processors with increasing numbers of qubits and improving error rates. However, the meaningful measure of progress isn't just qubit count, but the ability to maintain quantum coherence across larger systems for longer periods.

Recent demonstrations of "quantum supremacy"—performing specific calculations faster than classical computers—have shown that quantum computers can solve certain artificial problems exponentially faster than classical systems. However, extending these demonstrations to practical problems remains a significant challenge that will require continued advances in quantum hardware and algorithm development.

Quantum Programming and Algorithm Design

The Art of Quantum Algorithm Development

Designing quantum algorithms requires fundamentally different thinking than classical algorithm development. Classical algorithms specify deterministic sequences of operations that transform input data into desired outputs. Quantum algorithms must manipulate probabilistic quantum states to increase the likelihood that measurement yields correct answers while accounting for the inherent randomness of quantum mechanics.

Successful quantum algorithms typically follow common patterns that leverage quantum mechanical resources effectively. Many quantum algorithms begin by creating superposition states that enable parallel exploration of solution spaces. They then use quantum interference to amplify correct solutions while diminishing incorrect ones. Finally, they perform measurements designed to extract useful classical information from quantum calculations.

The development of quantum algorithms often requires insights from multiple disciplines. Algorithm designers must understand the mathematical structure of the problems they're trying to solve, the quantum mechanical principles that could provide computational advantages, and the practical limitations of current quantum hardware. This interdisciplinary nature makes quantum algorithm development both challenging and intellectually rewarding.

Quantum algorithms must also account for the limitations of current quantum hardware. Algorithms designed for perfect, noiseless quantum computers often perform poorly on current NISQ devices with significant error rates and limited coherence times. Practical quantum algorithm development requires balancing theoretical quantum advantages with the constraints imposed by noisy, limited quantum hardware.

Hybrid Classical-Quantum Approaches

Many current quantum algorithms use hybrid approaches that combine quantum and classical processing to solve problems more effectively than either approach alone. These hybrid algorithms typically use quantum computers to explore complex solution spaces while employing classical computers to optimize quantum parameters and process measurement results.

Variational quantum algorithms represent one important class of hybrid approaches. These algorithms use parameterized quantum circuits to prepare quantum states that encode problem solutions. Classical optimization algorithms adjust the quantum circuit parameters based on measurement results, gradually improving the quality of quantum solutions. This iterative approach can work with current noisy quantum hardware while potentially providing quantum advantages for optimization and machine learning problems.

The division of labor between quantum and classical components in hybrid algorithms requires careful consideration. Quantum computers excel at exploring exponentially large solution spaces and creating complex quantum correlations, while classical computers excel at precise numerical optimization and complex logical operations. Effective hybrid algorithms leverage the strengths of both computational paradigms while minimizing their respective weaknesses.

Hybrid approaches also provide a practical pathway for quantum computing adoption. Organizations can begin incorporating quantum components into their computational workflows without replacing their entire classical computing infrastructure. This gradual integration model may prove more practical than waiting for quantum computers that can replace classical systems entirely.

The Future Architecture

Modular Quantum Systems

The future of quantum computing likely involves modular architectures that combine multiple quantum processors through quantum communication links. Just as classical supercomputers achieve high performance by connecting many individual processors, large-scale quantum computers may consist of multiple quantum processing units connected by quantum networks.

Quantum modular architectures face unique challenges that don't exist in classical systems. Quantum information cannot be copied, making it difficult to distribute quantum calculations across multiple processors. Quantum communication links must preserve entanglement and superposition while transmitting quantum information between modules, requiring sophisticated quantum networking technologies.

The development of quantum networks for connecting quantum processors builds upon advances in quantum communication and quantum internet research. These networks must maintain quantum coherence over distances ranging from meters (within quantum computing systems) to potentially thousands of kilometers (for distributed quantum computing applications).

Error Correction at Scale

Future quantum computers will likely implement error correction hierarchically, with multiple levels of protection for quantum information. Low-level error correction will protect individual logical qubits using schemes like the surface code, while higher-level error correction will protect entire quantum algorithms from correlated errors that might affect multiple logical qubits simultaneously.

This hierarchical approach to error correction will require quantum computers to dedicate substantial resources to error detection and correction. Estimates suggest that 90% or more of a fault-tolerant quantum computer's qubits may be devoted to error correction rather than direct computation. This overhead highlights the importance of developing more efficient error correction schemes and improving the underlying fidelity of quantum operations.

The classical computational requirements for quantum error correction will also scale dramatically with quantum system size. Real-time processing of error syndrome information from millions of qubits will require powerful classical computers working in parallel with quantum processors. This classical-quantum integration represents a significant engineering challenge for large-scale quantum computing systems.

The journey from quantum mechanical phenomena to practical quantum computers reveals both the extraordinary ingenuity required to harness quantum effects for computation and the significant challenges that remain in building large-scale quantum systems. Understanding these building blocks—superposition, entanglement, quantum gates, and error correction—provides the foundation for appreciating both quantum computing's current capabilities and its future potential.

The strange properties of quantum mechanics that initially seemed like obstacles to practical application have become the very resources that enable quantum computational advantages. This transformation from fundamental physics to revolutionary technology continues to unfold as researchers develop more sophisticated quantum systems and algorithms. The next chapter will examine where quantum computing stands today, exploring the current capabilities and limitations of existing quantum computers as they begin to tackle real-world problems.

Chapter 4: The Current Landscape - Where We Stand Today

As we stand in 2025, quantum computing exists in a fascinating transitional phase that researchers call the "Noisy Intermediate-Scale Quantum" (NISQ) era. This period represents neither the early days of pure research nor the mature technology of fault-tolerant quantum computers, but something entirely unique—a time when quantum computers can demonstrate genuine quantum phenomena while remaining too limited and error-prone for most practical applications.

The current quantum computing landscape resembles the early days of classical computing in some ways, but with crucial differences. Where early classical computers were simply slower versions of modern machines, current quantum computers operate according to fundamentally different principles that both enable unique capabilities and impose severe limitations. Understanding this current state requires examining what quantum computers can and cannot do today, which technologies show the most promise, and how the major players in quantum computing are positioning themselves for the future.

Approximately 100 to 200 functional quantum computers exist worldwide as of 2025, with around 1,000 total quantum systems in various stages of development and testing. This small number reflects both the extraordinary technical challenges involved in building quantum computers and the specialized nature of current applications. Unlike classical computers, which became useful for a wide range of applications as they improved, quantum computers must overcome specific technical thresholds before they can provide practical advantages over classical systems.

The NISQ Era and Its Limitations

Defining the Current Moment

The NISQ era represents a unique period in quantum computing development where systems are large enough to perform interesting quantum calculations but too noisy and limited for fault-tolerant quantum computing. Current quantum computers typically contain between 50 and 1,000 qubits, sufficient to demonstrate quantum algorithms that cannot be simulated efficiently on classical computers, yet far from the millions of qubits that fully fault-tolerant systems will likely require.

The "noisy" designation reflects the high error rates that characterize current quantum computers. While classical computers achieve error rates of approximately one error per trillion operations, current quantum systems experience errors in roughly one out of every hundred to one thousand operations. These error rates limit quantum calculations to relatively short sequences of operations before accumulated errors destroy the quantum advantages that make these computations worthwhile.

Intermediate scale refers to the current qubit counts that occupy a middle ground between early proof-of-concept demonstrations and future large-scale systems. Current quantum computers have moved beyond the handful of qubits used in early experiments but remain orders of magnitude smaller than the systems that theoretical analysis suggests will be needed for transformative quantum applications.

The NISQ designation captures both the promise and the frustration of current quantum computing. These systems can perform calculations that would overwhelm classical computers, yet they cannot sustain the complex, long-running calculations needed for most practical applications. This limitation creates a race between improving quantum hardware capabilities and developing quantum algorithms that can provide value within current constraints.

Current Capabilities and Constraints

Modern quantum computers excel at specific types of problems while struggling with others that classical computers handle easily. Current systems can demonstrate quantum supremacy for carefully chosen problems—artificial computational tasks designed to showcase quantum advantages—but they cannot yet solve practical problems faster than classical computers for most real-world applications.

IBM's current Nighthawk hardware can execute quantum circuits containing up to 5,000 quantum gates, representing a significant increase from early systems that could handle only dozens of operations. However, this gate count remains far below the millions or billions of gates that complex quantum algorithms require. The limitation reflects both hardware constraints and the accumulation of errors as quantum circuits grow longer.

The coherence times of current qubits—the duration over which quantum states remain intact—typically range from microseconds to milliseconds depending on the physical implementation. These timescales allow for thousands of quantum operations but prevent the extended calculations that many practical quantum algorithms require. Improving coherence times represents one of the most important technical challenges in quantum computing development.

Current quantum computers also face significant constraints in qubit connectivity. Most quantum processors implement qubits in grid or linear arrangements where each qubit can interact directly with only a few neighbors. Quantum algorithms that require interactions between distant qubits must implement these connections through sequences of operations on intermediate qubits, increasing both computation time and error accumulation.

The Error Accumulation Challenge

The high error rates of current quantum computers create a fundamental tension in quantum algorithm design. Longer quantum calculations can solve more complex problems and potentially provide greater quantum advantages, but they also accumulate more errors that eventually overwhelm any quantum benefits. This trade-off forces quantum programmers to design algorithms that achieve useful results within the error budgets of current hardware.

Error accumulation in quantum computers differs qualitatively from error handling in classical systems. Classical computers can detect and correct most errors immediately, maintaining high fidelity throughout extended calculations. Quantum errors cannot be detected without destroying quantum information, requiring quantum error correction schemes that introduce substantial overhead and complexity.

The probabilistic nature of quantum computation compounds the error challenge. Even error-free quantum computers produce probabilistic results that require multiple runs to establish confidence in answers. When combined with hardware errors, determining whether unexpected results reflect genuine computational outcomes or accumulated errors becomes challenging.

Current quantum computing research focuses heavily on developing error mitigation techniques that can extract useful results from noisy quantum calculations. These techniques include zero-noise extrapolation, symmetry verification, and error mitigation through classical post-processing. While these approaches cannot eliminate quantum errors, they can extend the useful range of current quantum hardware.

Leading Quantum Technologies

Superconducting Quantum Systems

Superconducting qubits currently dominate commercial quantum computing platforms, powering systems from IBM, Google, Rigetti, and numerous other companies. These qubits operate using Josephson junctions—quantum mechanical devices that allow electrical current to flow without resistance at temperatures near absolute zero. The solid-state nature of superconducting qubits enables fabrication using semiconductor manufacturing techniques, potentially allowing for large-scale production as the technology matures.

IBM has established itself as a leader in superconducting quantum systems, with their roadmap targeting quantum-centric supercomputers containing over 4,000 qubits by 2025. Their modular approach allows multiple quantum processors to be connected through classical and quantum communication links, enabling scaling beyond the limits of individual quantum chips. The IBM Quantum System Two can support configurations with up to 16,632 qubits when multiple processors are networked together.

Google's superconducting quantum processors have achieved some of the most dramatic demonstrations of quantum computational advantages. Their Sycamore processor gained worldwide attention by demonstrating quantum supremacy for specific computational tasks, showing that quantum computers could solve certain problems exponentially faster than classical systems. Google's recent Willow chip represents continued advancement in superconducting qubit technology, with improved error rates and coherence times.

However, superconducting quantum computers face significant practical challenges. They require dilution refrigerators that cool qubits to temperatures below 10 millikelvin—colder than outer space. These cooling systems are expensive, energy-intensive, and require specialized maintenance. The extreme operating conditions limit where superconducting quantum computers can be deployed and increase their operational complexity.

Trapped Ion Excellence

Trapped ion quantum computers represent the current state-of-the-art in quantum coherence and gate fidelity. These systems use individual ions confined by electromagnetic fields as qubits, achieving coherence times measured in minutes rather than the microseconds typical of superconducting systems. The exceptional stability of trapped ion qubits enables high-fidelity quantum operations that approach the theoretical limits of quantum gate accuracy.

IonQ has emerged as a leader in trapped ion quantum computing, developing systems that consistently achieve the highest quantum volume metrics—composite measures of quantum computer capability that account for qubit count, connectivity, and error rates. Their trapped ion systems can perform quantum operations with fidelities exceeding 99.8%, substantially better than most other quantum computing approaches.

Quantinuum, formed from the merger of Honeywell Quantum Solutions and Cambridge Quantum Computing, has developed trapped ion systems that demonstrate some of the most sophisticated quantum algorithms to date. Their H-Series quantum computers have achieved quantum volume records and demonstrated quantum algorithms for chemistry, optimization, and machine learning applications.

The primary limitation of trapped ion systems lies in their operational speed. Individual quantum gates in trapped ion systems typically require microseconds to complete, compared to nanoseconds for superconducting qubits. This speed difference means that trapped ion systems must rely on their superior coherence and fidelity to compensate for slower gate operations. For algorithms requiring many sequential operations, this trade-off can limit the practical advantages of trapped ion approaches.

Photonic Quantum Computing

Photonic quantum computers encode quantum information in individual photons, offering unique advantages for quantum communication and certain types of quantum computation. Photonic systems can operate at room temperature and naturally resist many sources of environmental interference that plague other quantum computing approaches. These characteristics make photonic quantum computers attractive for applications requiring quantum communication or integration with classical optical systems.

PsiQuantum has pursued an ambitious approach to photonic quantum computing, developing systems designed to achieve fault-tolerant quantum computation using millions of photonic qubits. Their approach relies on photonic fusion gates and quantum error correction specifically designed for photonic systems. While challenging to implement, this approach could potentially skip the NISQ era entirely and move directly to fault-tolerant quantum computing.

Xanadu has developed photonic quantum computers based on continuous variable quantum computing, where quantum information is encoded in the quantum properties of light fields rather than discrete photon states. Their X-Series quantum computers can be programmed using conventional programming languages and demonstrate quantum algorithms for optimization and machine learning applications.

The primary challenge for photonic quantum computing lies in implementing the nonlinear interactions needed for universal quantum computation. Photons typically don't interact with each other directly, requiring complex optical systems and auxiliary components to create the quantum gates necessary for general-purpose quantum computation. Recent advances in photonic quantum computing have demonstrated promising approaches to overcoming these limitations.

Emerging Technologies

Neutral atom quantum computers have emerged as a promising alternative approach that combines advantages of trapped ion systems with potentially better scalability. Companies like Pasqal and Atom Computing use optical tweezers to trap individual atoms and manipulate them using precisely controlled laser pulses. These systems can create flexible qubit connectivity patterns and demonstrate impressive coherence properties.

Silicon quantum dots represent another emerging approach that leverages semiconductor manufacturing expertise to build quantum computers. Intel has invested heavily in silicon quantum computing, developing qubits based on quantum dots and silicon-based fabrication processes. This approach could potentially leverage existing semiconductor manufacturing infrastructure to scale quantum computer production.

Topological qubits, pursued by Microsoft and other research organizations, aim to create qubits that are inherently protected from certain types of errors. These qubits would encode quantum information in topological properties of quantum systems that are naturally resistant to local perturbations. While still largely experimental, topological qubits could provide a pathway to more robust quantum computing if successful.

Major Players and Their Approaches

IBM's Quantum Leadership

IBM has positioned itself as the clear leader in quantum computing accessibility and education through its comprehensive quantum computing ecosystem. The IBM Quantum Network includes over 200 academic institutions, research laboratories, and companies worldwide, providing access to IBM's quantum systems and fostering quantum computing research and development.

IBM's technical roadmap emphasizes modular quantum computing architectures that can scale beyond the limitations of individual quantum processors. Their approach involves connecting multiple quantum processing units through quantum communication links, enabling distributed quantum computations that can tackle problems requiring more qubits than single processors can provide.

The company's quantum software stack, Qiskit, has become one of the most widely used quantum programming platforms. Qiskit provides tools for quantum circuit design, algorithm optimization, and error mitigation that work across different quantum hardware platforms. This software leadership has positioned IBM as a central hub for quantum computing development even beyond their own hardware platforms.

IBM's emphasis on quantum error mitigation and correction represents their pathway toward fault-tolerant quantum computing. Their research in quantum error correction has demonstrated some of the most advanced error mitigation techniques available today, and their roadmap includes specific milestones for implementing logical qubits with error correction. By 2029, IBM expects to execute quantum circuits containing 100 million quantum gates—a 20,000-fold increase over current capabilities.

Google's Quantum AI Vision

Google approaches quantum computing through their Quantum AI division, which focuses on using quantum computers to accelerate artificial intelligence and solve scientific computing problems. Their 2019 demonstration of quantum supremacy using the 53-qubit Sycamore processor marked a crucial milestone in proving that quantum computers could outperform classical systems for specific tasks.

Google's quantum roadmap aims for useful, error-corrected quantum computers by 2029, building on their demonstrated ability to achieve quantum supremacy. Their approach emphasizes logical qubits—error-corrected qubits that can perform reliable quantum operations—as the pathway to practical quantum computing. Recent work with their Willow chip has demonstrated progress toward this goal, showing error reduction through increased physical qubit resources.

The company's substantial investment in quantum computing research, totaling billions of dollars over the past decade, reflects their conviction that quantum computers will transform artificial intelligence and scientific computing. CEO Sundar Pichai has emphasized quantum computing's potential role in addressing global challenges like climate change and drug discovery, predicting transformative impacts within five to ten years.

Google's quantum research benefits from integration with their broader artificial intelligence research efforts. The company investigates how quantum computers could accelerate machine learning algorithms, optimize neural network training, and solve computational problems that arise in AI development. This integrated approach positions Google to capture synergies between quantum computing and artificial intelligence as both technologies mature.

Microsoft's Software-First Strategy

Microsoft has pursued a distinctive approach to quantum computing that emphasizes software development and quantum programming tools over hardware development. Their Azure Quantum cloud platform provides access to quantum computers from multiple hardware vendors, positioning Microsoft as a quantum software and services provider rather than a hardware manufacturer.

The company's Q# quantum programming language and development tools aim to make quantum programming more accessible to classical software developers. Microsoft's approach abstracts away many hardware-specific details, allowing programmers to focus on algorithm development rather than the intricacies of particular quantum hardware platforms.

Microsoft's research in topological quantum computing represents their long-term hardware strategy. Topological qubits could provide inherent protection against certain types of quantum errors, potentially enabling more robust quantum computers. While this approach remains largely experimental, successful development of topological qubits could provide Microsoft with a significant competitive advantage in quantum hardware.

The company's quantum computing efforts integrate closely with their cloud computing and artificial intelligence services. Microsoft envisions quantum computing as a natural extension of their cloud platform, providing quantum capabilities alongside classical computing resources. This integrated approach could accelerate quantum computing adoption by making quantum resources available through familiar cloud interfaces.

Amazon's Quantum Services Platform

Amazon has entered quantum computing through their Braket cloud service, which provides access to quantum computers from multiple vendors through a single platform interface. This approach leverages Amazon's cloud computing expertise while avoiding the substantial investments required for quantum hardware development.

Braket supports quantum computers from IonQ, Rigetti, D-Wave, and other hardware providers, allowing customers to compare different quantum computing approaches and choose optimal systems for specific applications. The platform includes quantum simulators that enable algorithm development and testing without requiring access to physical quantum hardware.

Amazon's quantum computing strategy also includes the Center for Quantum Computing at Caltech, a research collaboration focused on developing fault-tolerant quantum computers. This research partnership allows Amazon to contribute to fundamental quantum computing research while building expertise for future quantum services.

The company's approach reflects their conviction that quantum computing will follow a similar trajectory to classical cloud computing, where specialized providers offer quantum capabilities as cloud services rather than requiring customers to own and operate quantum hardware directly. This service-oriented model could accelerate quantum computing adoption by reducing barriers to entry for organizations interested in exploring quantum applications.

Current Quantum Computing Trends

The quantum computing field in 2025 is characterized by six major trends that are shaping its development trajectory. First, increased experimentation with logical qubits—error-corrected qubits that can perform reliable quantum operations—represents progress toward fault-tolerant quantum computing. These experiments demonstrate that quantum error correction can work in practice, though current implementations still require substantial overhead.

Second, the development of specialized quantum hardware and software for specific applications, rather than universal quantum computers, shows growing maturity in the field. Companies are recognizing that different quantum computing approaches excel at different types of problems, leading to more targeted development efforts that match quantum capabilities to application requirements.

Third, networking NISQ devices together to create more powerful distributed quantum systems represents an important scaling strategy. Since building larger individual quantum processors faces significant technical challenges, connecting multiple smaller systems through quantum communication links provides an alternative pathway to increased quantum computing capability.

Fourth, the development of software abstraction layers makes quantum programming more accessible to developers without deep quantum mechanics expertise. These tools hide the complexity of quantum hardware while providing access to quantum computational capabilities, similar to how high-level programming languages abstract away the details of classical computer hardware.

Fifth, workforce development tools and educational resources are expanding rapidly as universities and companies recognize the need for quantum-literate workers. The growing availability of quantum computing courses, certification programs, and hands-on learning platforms reflects the industry's recognition that human capital development is as important as technological advancement.

Sixth, continued improvements in physical qubit implementations across all major quantum computing approaches demonstrate ongoing progress in the fundamental building blocks of quantum computers. These improvements include longer coherence times, higher gate fidelities, and better qubit connectivity, all of which directly impact the capabilities of quantum computing systems.

Leading Quantum Technologies

Superconducting Quantum Processors

Superconducting quantum computers have achieved the most dramatic demonstrations of quantum computational power, including Google's quantum supremacy demonstration and IBM's growing portfolio of cloud-accessible quantum processors. These systems use superconducting circuits operating at millikelvin temperatures to create qubits that can be manipulated using microwave pulses with nanosecond precision.

The primary advantages of superconducting qubits include fast gate operations, well-developed fabrication techniques based on semiconductor manufacturing, and good integration with classical electronics. IBM's quantum processors achieve gate times of tens of nanoseconds, enabling thousands of quantum operations within typical coherence windows. The solid-state nature of superconducting qubits also enables precise control and measurement using established electronic techniques.

Current superconducting quantum computers face limitations in qubit connectivity and error rates. Most superconducting processors implement qubits in grid patterns where each qubit connects to only a few neighbors, requiring additional operations to implement quantum algorithms that need interactions between distant qubits. Two-qubit gate error rates typically range from 0.1% to 1%, limiting the depth of quantum circuits that can be executed reliably.

The roadmap for superconducting quantum computing focuses on increasing qubit counts, improving error rates, and developing modular architectures that can scale beyond single-chip limitations. IBM's quantum roadmap targets quantum-centric supercomputers with thousands of qubits by the late 2020s, achieved through networking multiple quantum processors together.

Trapped Ion Precision

Trapped ion quantum computers achieve the highest fidelity quantum operations currently available, with single-qubit and two-qubit gates regularly exceeding 99.9% and 99.8% fidelity respectively. These exceptional error rates reflect the exquisite control possible over individual ions confined in electromagnetic traps and manipulated using precisely controlled laser pulses.

IonQ and Quantinuum lead the development of trapped ion quantum computers, with systems that demonstrate some of the most sophisticated quantum algorithms implemented to date. Trapped ion systems can implement quantum gates between any pair of qubits, providing full connectivity that simplifies quantum algorithm implementation compared to grid-based architectures.

The exceptional coherence properties of trapped ion qubits enable quantum calculations that would be impossible on other current quantum computing platforms. Coherence times measured in minutes allow for quantum algorithms requiring thousands of operations, opening applications that remain inaccessible to faster but less coherent quantum computing approaches.

However, trapped ion quantum computers operate more slowly than superconducting systems, with gate times measured in microseconds rather than nanoseconds. This speed limitation means that trapped ion systems must rely on their superior coherence and fidelity to provide quantum advantages, particularly for applications requiring high-precision quantum operations over extended periods.

Photonic Innovation

Photonic quantum computing has made remarkable progress in addressing the fundamental challenges that initially limited this approach. Xanadu's X-Series processors demonstrate room-temperature quantum computing using photonic qubits, eliminating the expensive cooling requirements that constrain other quantum computing approaches.

The development of photonic fusion gates and error correction schemes specifically designed for photonic systems has addressed previous limitations in creating universal photonic quantum computers. PsiQuantum's approach to fault-tolerant photonic quantum computing aims to build systems with millions of qubits that could skip the NISQ era entirely and move directly to error-corrected quantum computation.

Photonic quantum computers offer unique advantages for quantum communication and networking applications. Photons naturally serve as excellent carriers of quantum information over long distances, enabling photonic quantum computers to integrate seamlessly with quantum communication networks. This integration capability positions photonic systems well for distributed quantum computing applications.

The primary remaining challenge for photonic quantum computing involves scaling to the large numbers of components required for universal quantum computation. Current photonic quantum computers require complex optical systems with thousands of precisely aligned components, creating engineering challenges in building large-scale photonic quantum processors.

Neutral Atom Flexibility

Neutral atom quantum computers have emerged as a promising approach that combines the best features of trapped ion and superconducting systems. Companies like Pasqal and Atom Computing use optical tweezers to trap neutral atoms and manipulate them using laser pulses, achieving good coherence properties while maintaining reasonable gate speeds.

The flexibility of neutral atom systems represents their primary advantage. Optical tweezers can be reconfigured dynamically to create different qubit connectivity patterns, enabling quantum algorithms that require complex interaction topologies. This reconfigurability allows neutral atom systems to optimize their configuration for different quantum algorithms.

Neutral atom systems also demonstrate impressive scaling properties. Recent demonstrations have shown neutral atom quantum computers with hundreds of qubits, and the optical trapping techniques appear capable of scaling to thousands of qubits. The ability to load qubits into arbitrary two- and three-dimensional arrangements provides additional flexibility for quantum algorithm implementation.

Current limitations of neutral atom quantum computing include the complexity of optical control systems and challenges in achieving uniform performance across large arrays of trapped atoms. However, rapid progress in this field suggests that neutral atom systems could become significant players in the quantum computing landscape as the technology matures.

As we examine the current quantum computing landscape, we see a field in rapid transition from research curiosity to practical technology. The NISQ era represents both the promise and the challenge of current quantum computing—systems powerful enough to demonstrate genuine quantum advantages but limited enough to require careful algorithm design and error management. The diversity of quantum computing approaches reflects the field's continued exploration of the best pathways to practical quantum computing applications.

Chapter 5: The Global Race - Nations and Corporations Competing for Quantum Supremacy

The quantum computing revolution has triggered one of the most intense technological competitions in modern history, comparable to the space race of the 1960s or the internet development of the 1990s. Nations around the world recognize that quantum computing represents a strategic technology that could determine economic competitiveness, national security capabilities, and scientific leadership for decades to come. This recognition has sparked massive government investments, aggressive corporate research programs, and a global talent war as countries and companies race to achieve quantum advantages.

The stakes of this competition extend far beyond technological bragging rights. Quantum computers promise to revolutionize fields from drug discovery to artificial intelligence, potentially creating trillions of dollars in economic value. Simultaneously, these same machines threaten to render current cryptographic systems obsolete, potentially destabilizing the digital infrastructure that underlies modern commerce and communication. The nations and companies that lead in quantum computing development will shape how these transformative technologies affect global economics, security, and scientific progress.

Unlike previous technological competitions that primarily involved private companies or individual nations, the quantum race involves complex interactions between governments, corporations, universities, and international collaborations. Success requires not just technological innovation, but also substantial financial resources, specialized infrastructure, and access to highly skilled researchers. The global nature of quantum research creates both collaborative opportunities and competitive tensions as nations balance open scientific cooperation with national security concerns.

Government Investments and National Strategies

The United States Quantum Initiative

The United States has approached quantum computing as a national priority requiring coordinated federal investment and strategic planning. The National Quantum Initiative Act, signed into law in 2018, authorized over $ 1.2 billion in federal funding for quantum research and established a coordinated national strategy for quantum technology development. This legislation created quantum research institutes, funded basic research at universities and national laboratories, and established workforce development programs to train the next generation of quantum researchers.

The U.S. approach emphasizes collaboration between government agencies, universities, and private companies through initiatives like the Quantum Economic Development Consortium (QED-C) and the Quantum Information Science Research Centers. These partnerships aim to accelerate the transition from laboratory research to commercial applications while maintaining American leadership in quantum technology development.

Defense and intelligence agencies have made quantum computing a strategic priority, recognizing both the opportunities and threats that quantum technology presents. The Department of Defense has established quantum computing research programs focused on applications ranging from optimization and simulation to quantum sensing and communication. The intelligence community has invested heavily in understanding how quantum computers might affect cryptographic security and intelligence gathering capabilities.

The National Science Foundation, Department of Energy, and other federal agencies have created quantum computing research programs that support both fundamental research and application development. These programs fund university research, national laboratory projects, and small business innovation research that spans the full spectrum of quantum computing development from basic science to commercial applications.

China's Quantum Ambitions

China has made quantum technology a central component of its national strategy for technological leadership, with investments that may exceed all other nations combined. The Chinese government has announced quantum computing investments totaling tens of billions of dollars, establishing research institutes, funding university programs, and supporting both state-owned and private quantum computing companies.

The University of Science and Technology of China (USTC) has achieved several quantum computing milestones, including demonstrations of quantum supremacy using photonic quantum computers. Their Jiuzhang quantum computer demonstrated quantum advantages for specific computational problems, complementing superconducting quantum computing demonstrations from other research groups.

China's approach to quantum computing development emphasizes both fundamental research and practical applications. The government has established quantum computing research centers in major cities, funded large-scale quantum computing projects, and created educational programs to develop quantum computing expertise. This comprehensive approach aims to ensure that China can compete across all aspects of quantum technology development.

The geopolitical implications of China's quantum computing investments have prompted concerns in other nations about the security implications of quantum technology. The potential for quantum computers to break current encryption systems has made quantum computing a matter of national security, leading to export controls and technology transfer restrictions that affect international quantum computing collaboration.

European Union's Quantum Flagship

The European Union has launched the Quantum Flagship, a €1 billion research initiative designed to coordinate quantum technology development across European nations. This program aims to maintain European competitiveness in quantum technologies while fostering collaboration between European research institutions and companies.

The Quantum Flagship emphasizes quantum communication and quantum sensing applications alongside quantum computing, reflecting Europe's strengths in these areas. European companies and research institutions have achieved leadership positions in quantum cryptography and quantum sensing, technologies that complement quantum computing and could provide near-term commercial applications.

European quantum computing research benefits from strong academic institutions and established physics research traditions. Countries like Germany, the Netherlands, and Austria have long histories of quantum physics research that provide foundations for quantum computing development. The European approach leverages these existing strengths while building new capabilities in quantum engineering and applications.

However, the European quantum computing effort faces challenges in competing with the scale of investments from the United States and China. The fragmented nature of European research funding and the need to coordinate across multiple national governments can slow decision-making and resource allocation compared to more centralized approaches in other regions.

Other National Initiatives

Canada has established itself as an early leader in quantum computing through companies like D-Wave Systems and Xanadu, combined with strong university research programs and government support for quantum technology development. The Canadian government has invested hundreds of millions of dollars in quantum research and has created quantum computing clusters in cities like Toronto and Vancouver.

Australia has launched a National Quantum Commercialisation Hub and invested heavily in quantum technology research through universities and government research organizations. Australian researchers have made significant contributions to quantum error correction and quantum algorithm development, while Australian companies are developing quantum software and applications.

Japan has created quantum computing research programs through organizations like RIKEN and has established partnerships with international quantum computing companies. The Japanese government has announced substantial investments in quantum technology as part of broader efforts to maintain technological competitiveness in emerging technologies.

The United Kingdom leverages its strong quantum physics research tradition through the National Quantum Computing Centre and substantial government investments in quantum technology. British researchers have made fundamental contributions to quantum computing theory and experimental implementation, while UK companies are developing quantum software and applications.

Tech Giants and Their Quantum Ambitions

IBM's Comprehensive Ecosystem

IBM has built the most comprehensive quantum computing ecosystem in the industry, combining hardware development, software platforms, cloud services, and educational programs. Their quantum computing strategy extends beyond building quantum processors to creating the entire infrastructure needed for quantum computing adoption, from programming tools to workforce development.

The IBM Quantum Network has become the largest quantum computing collaboration in the world, including Fortune 500 companies, startups, universities, and government research laboratories. This network provides members with access to IBM's quantum systems while fostering research collaboration and quantum computing education. The breadth of this network gives IBM unique insights into quantum computing applications across diverse industries.

IBM's quantum roadmap reflects their systematic approach to scaling quantum computing capabilities. Their target of quantum-centric supercomputers containing over 4,000 qubits by 2025 represents ambitious but achievable goals based on their current technological trajectory. The modular architecture underlying these systems could enable scaling to even larger systems as quantum networking technologies mature.

The company's emphasis on quantum software development positions them well for the transition from NISQ devices to fault-tolerant quantum computers. Their Qiskit platform has become a de facto standard for quantum programming, providing them with valuable data about quantum algorithm development and user requirements that will inform future quantum computing development.

Google's AI-Quantum Integration

Google's approach to quantum computing reflects their broader strategy of using advanced computing technologies to accelerate artificial intelligence development. Their Quantum AI division focuses specifically on applications where quantum computers could provide advantages for machine learning, optimization, and scientific simulation problems that arise in AI research.

The company's demonstration of quantum supremacy in 2019 established their technical credibility while generating substantial media attention and public interest in quantum computing. This achievement helped validate the quantum computing field and accelerated investment and interest from other technology companies.

Google's quantum research benefits from integration with their broader research efforts in artificial intelligence, machine learning, and scientific computing. The company can leverage their expertise in these areas to identify quantum computing applications and develop hybrid classical-quantum algorithms that combine the strengths of both computational approaches.

Their quantum roadmap emphasizes logical qubits and error correction as the pathway to practical quantum computing applications. The target of useful, error-corrected quantum computers by 2029 reflects ambitious goals that could position Google as a leader in the transition from NISQ devices to fault-tolerant quantum computing.

Microsoft's Platform Strategy

Microsoft has positioned itself as the platform provider for quantum computing, similar to their successful strategy in classical computing software. Azure Quantum provides access to quantum computers from multiple hardware vendors while offering quantum development tools, simulators, and programming languages that work across different quantum platforms.

The company's investment in topological quantum computing represents a long-term bet on a potentially superior approach to quantum hardware. While topological qubits remain largely experimental, successful development could provide Microsoft with significant competitive advantages in quantum hardware. Their research partnership with academic institutions and government laboratories strengthens their position in this emerging area.

Microsoft's quantum programming tools, including the Q# language and quantum development kit, aim to make quantum programming accessible to the millions of developers familiar with Microsoft's software platforms. This approach could accelerate quantum computing adoption by leveraging existing developer communities rather than requiring entirely new quantum programming expertise.

The integration of quantum computing capabilities with Microsoft's cloud computing and artificial intelligence services creates opportunities for hybrid applications that combine classical and quantum processing. This integrated approach could provide competitive advantages as quantum computing transitions from specialized research tools to general-purpose computing resources.

Amazon's Service-Oriented Approach

Amazon's entry into quantum computing through cloud services reflects their expertise in platform businesses and their recognition that quantum computing may follow a similar adoption pattern to classical cloud computing. Braket provides customers with access to diverse quantum computing technologies while abstracting away the complexity of managing quantum hardware directly.

The platform approach allows Amazon to benefit from quantum computing advances without making large investments in specific quantum hardware technologies. By supporting multiple quantum computing approaches, Amazon can adapt their services as the field evolves and customer preferences become clearer.

Amazon's quantum computing strategy also includes substantial research investments through partnerships with academic institutions and government research laboratories. The Center for Quantum Computing at Caltech focuses on developing fault-tolerant quantum computers while building Amazon's internal quantum computing expertise.

The company's approach positions them well for the transition from current NISQ devices to future fault-tolerant quantum computers. Their cloud platform can incorporate new quantum technologies as they become available while providing consistent interfaces for customers developing quantum applications.

Startups Disrupting the Field

Hardware Innovation Leaders

The quantum computing startup ecosystem has produced numerous innovative companies that are pushing the boundaries of quantum hardware development. Rigetti Computing has developed cloud-accessible superconducting quantum computers while also offering quantum cloud services that compete with larger technology companies. Their focus on practical quantum computing applications has attracted customers from finance, logistics, and optimization sectors.

IonQ has emerged as the leader in trapped ion quantum computing, achieving some of the highest quantum computing performance metrics available today. Their systems consistently demonstrate superior quantum volume—a composite measure of quantum computer capability—and have attracted significant investment from both venture capital and strategic investors.

Atom Computing has developed neutral atom quantum computers with some of the largest qubit counts currently available, demonstrating systems with over 1,000 qubits. Their approach using optical tweezers to trap and manipulate individual atoms provides flexibility in qubit connectivity while maintaining good coherence properties.

PsiQuantum has pursued an ambitious approach to photonic quantum computing, aiming to build fault-tolerant quantum computers with millions of qubits. Their photonic approach could potentially skip the NISQ era entirely, though it requires overcoming significant technical challenges in photonic quantum error correction and gate implementation.

Software and Algorithm Specialists

Quantum computing software startups have created specialized tools and algorithms that enhance the capabilities of quantum hardware platforms. Cambridge Quantum Computing (now part of Quantinuum) developed quantum software tools and algorithms for chemistry, optimization, and machine learning applications. Their focus on practical quantum algorithms has demonstrated some of the most sophisticated quantum computing applications to date.

Menten AI applies quantum computing to drug discovery and protein design, using quantum algorithms to solve molecular optimization problems that are intractable for classical computers. Their approach demonstrates how quantum computing can address practical problems in pharmaceutical research and biotechnology.

Rahko (acquired by Odyssey Therapeutics) used quantum machine learning algorithms for drug discovery, showing how quantum computing could accelerate pharmaceutical research. Their work illustrates the potential for quantum computing to impact life sciences through improved molecular modeling and drug optimization.

ProteinQure applies quantum computing to molecular simulation and drug discovery, using quantum algorithms to predict molecular properties and optimize pharmaceutical compounds. Their platform demonstrates practical applications of quantum computing in chemistry and pharmaceutical research.

Quantum Communication and Networking

Quantum communication startups are developing the networking technologies that will enable distributed quantum computing and quantum internet applications. ID Quantique has commercialized quantum key distribution systems that provide unbreakable cryptographic security using quantum mechanical principles.

Quantum Xchange has developed quantum key distribution networks for securing critical communications infrastructure, providing quantum-enhanced security for financial services, government communications, and other high-security applications. Their networks demonstrate practical implementations of quantum communication technology.

SpeQtral focuses on satellite-based quantum communication, developing space-based quantum key distribution systems that could enable global quantum communication networks. Their approach addresses the distance limitations of terrestrial quantum communication by using satellites as quantum communication nodes.

The quantum startup ecosystem reflects the diverse opportunities and approaches in quantum technology development. From hardware innovation to software applications to communication networks, startups are exploring every aspect of quantum technology while competing with established technology giants and government research programs.

The competitive landscape in quantum computing continues to evolve rapidly as new technologies emerge and existing approaches mature. The success of different companies and countries will depend not just on their technical achievements, but on their ability to translate quantum computing capabilities into practical applications that provide real-world value. This race for quantum advantage will ultimately determine how quantum computing transforms our technological landscape and which organizations capture the benefits of this revolutionary technology.

The global competition in quantum computing has created an environment of unprecedented innovation and investment. As we'll explore in the next chapter, this competitive pressure is driving the development of quantum applications that promise to revolutionize industries from healthcare to finance, while simultaneously creating new challenges and opportunities that will reshape our technological future.

Chapter 6: The Promise - Revolutionary Applications on the Horizon

The quantum computing revolution promises to transform entire industries by solving problems that have remained intractable despite decades of advances in classical computing power. While current quantum computers operate in the noisy intermediate-scale quantum era with significant limitations, the applications emerging from early research provide glimpses of a future where quantum computers tackle humanity's most challenging computational problems. From discovering life-saving medications to modeling climate systems with unprecedented accuracy, quantum computing could reshape how we approach scientific discovery, business optimization, and technological innovation.

The promise of quantum computing extends beyond mere computational speedup—it represents a fundamentally different approach to solving complex problems that involve quantum mechanical phenomena, optimization across vast solution spaces, and pattern recognition in high-dimensional data. As quantum hardware continues to improve and error correction advances toward fault-tolerant systems, these applications will transition from promising research directions to transformative commercial technologies that could impact billions of lives.

Current quantum computing revenue of 650–750millionisprojectedtoexceed650–750*millionisprojectedtoexceed* 1 billion in 2025, reflecting growing confidence in near-term quantum applications. While this represents a small fraction of the classical computing market, the exponential growth trajectory and the transformative potential of quantum applications suggest that quantum computing could reshape entire economic sectors within the next decade.

Drug Discovery and Medical Breakthroughs

Molecular Simulation Revolution

The pharmaceutical industry faces one of the most computationally challenging problems in modern science: understanding how molecules interact at the quantum level to create biological effects. Drug discovery currently requires testing millions of potential compounds through expensive laboratory experiments, with most candidates failing during clinical trials after years of development and billions of dollars in investment. Quantum computers promise to revolutionize this process by enabling accurate molecular simulation that could identify promising drug candidates before expensive laboratory testing begins.

Classical computers struggle with molecular simulation because molecules are fundamentally quantum mechanical systems. When scientists try to predict how a potential drug molecule will bind to a target protein, they must account for quantum effects including electron behavior, chemical bonding, and molecular vibrations. The computational requirements for accurate molecular simulation grow exponentially with molecular size, quickly overwhelming even the most powerful classical supercomputers.

Quantum computers offer a natural solution to molecular simulation challenges because both the computer and the molecules being studied operate according to quantum mechanical principles. Richard Feynman's original vision of quantum computing emphasized this natural match between quantum computers and quantum systems. A quantum computer simulating molecular behavior doesn't need to translate quantum phenomena into classical calculations—it can model quantum systems directly using its own quantum properties.

Early demonstrations of quantum molecular simulation have shown promising results for small molecules, and researchers predict that quantum computers could simulate pharmaceutically relevant molecules within the next decade. Companies like Menten AI and ProteinQure are already applying early quantum computing techniques to drug discovery, demonstrating practical applications of quantum molecular simulation in pharmaceutical research.

The potential impact of quantum-enhanced drug discovery extends far beyond the pharmaceutical industry. Faster drug development could accelerate treatments for diseases affecting millions of people, reduce healthcare costs by bringing medications to market more quickly, and enable personalized medicine approaches that tailor treatments to individual genetic profiles. The COVID-19 pandemic highlighted the critical importance of rapid drug development, and quantum computing could provide tools for responding more quickly to future health emergencies.

Protein Folding and Structural Biology

Understanding how proteins fold into their functional three-dimensional structures represents one of biology's greatest unsolved problems. Proteins are complex molecules that must fold into precise shapes to perform their biological functions, but predicting these folded structures from protein sequences remains extraordinarily difficult. Classical approaches to protein folding prediction require massive computational resources and often fail for large, complex proteins.

Quantum computers could revolutionize protein structure prediction by modeling the quantum mechanical forces that govern protein folding. The weak interactions between amino acids that determine protein structure involve quantum effects that are difficult to capture accurately using classical simulation methods. Quantum computers could model these interactions more directly, potentially enabling accurate prediction of protein structures that remain unsolved despite decades of research effort.

The implications of solving protein folding extend throughout medical research and biotechnology. Understanding protein structures enables rational drug design, where medications are designed to interact with specific protein binding sites. Protein structure prediction also supports the development of new enzymes for industrial applications, therapeutic proteins for treating genetic diseases, and diagnostic tools for detecting disease-related protein changes.

Recent advances in AI-powered protein folding prediction, exemplified by DeepMind's AlphaFold system, have demonstrated remarkable progress using classical computers and machine learning. However, these approaches still struggle with dynamic protein behavior, protein-protein interactions, and the effects of different cellular environments on protein structure. Quantum computers could complement these AI approaches by providing more accurate modeling of the quantum mechanical phenomena underlying protein behavior.

Personalized Medicine and Genomics

Quantum computing could enable personalized medicine approaches that tailor treatments to individual patients based on their genetic profiles, molecular characteristics, and disease progression. Current personalized medicine faces computational limitations in analyzing the vast amounts of genomic and molecular data needed to optimize individual treatments. Quantum computers could process this data more effectively, identifying patterns and correlations that classical analysis might miss.

Genomic data analysis presents computational challenges that align well with quantum computing capabilities. The human genome contains billions of base pairs, and understanding how genetic variations affect disease risk and treatment response requires analyzing complex patterns across this vast dataset. Quantum algorithms could potentially identify genetic signatures associated with specific diseases or treatment responses more efficiently than classical approaches.

Drug metabolism prediction represents another area where quantum computing could enable personalized medicine. Understanding how individual patients metabolize specific medications requires modeling complex biochemical pathways that involve quantum mechanical processes. Quantum computers could simulate these pathways more accurately, enabling personalized dosing and reducing adverse drug reactions.

The integration of quantum computing with electronic health records and real-time patient monitoring could enable dynamic treatment optimization that adapts to changing patient conditions. This approach could improve treatment outcomes while reducing healthcare costs by avoiding ineffective treatments and minimizing adverse reactions.

Climate Modeling and Environmental Solutions

Advanced Weather and Climate Prediction

Climate modeling represents one of the most computationally demanding challenges facing humanity today. Current climate models require massive supercomputers to simulate atmospheric, oceanic, and terrestrial processes at global scales. Despite these substantial computational resources, climate models still struggle to capture fine-scale phenomena that significantly affect regional weather patterns and long-term climate trends.

Quantum computers could revolutionize climate modeling by enabling more accurate simulation of molecular-scale processes that affect atmospheric chemistry, cloud formation, and energy transfer. Current climate models must approximate these processes using simplified equations, but quantum computers could potentially model the underlying quantum mechanical phenomena more directly.

The chaotic nature of atmospheric systems presents particular challenges for classical climate modeling. Small changes in initial conditions can lead to dramatically different weather outcomes, requiring climate models to explore many possible scenarios to provide reliable predictions. Quantum computers could potentially explore these scenario spaces more efficiently, providing more accurate probabilistic weather forecasts.

Quantum-enhanced climate modeling could improve predictions of extreme weather events, which have become increasingly important as climate change increases the frequency and intensity of hurricanes, droughts, and other extreme conditions. Better predictions could save lives and reduce economic damage by enabling more effective preparation and response to extreme weather events.

Carbon Capture and Environmental Chemistry

Developing effective technologies for removing carbon dioxide from the atmosphere requires understanding complex chemical processes that could benefit from quantum simulation. Current carbon capture technologies face efficiency and cost challenges that limit their deployment at the scales needed to address climate change. Quantum computers could accelerate the development of more effective carbon capture materials and processes.

Catalysis—the process of accelerating chemical reactions using specialized materials—plays a crucial role in many environmental technologies. Designing better catalysts for carbon capture, renewable energy production, and pollution control requires understanding quantum mechanical processes that govern how molecules interact with catalyst surfaces. Quantum computers could model these interactions more accurately than classical approaches.

The development of new materials for solar cells, batteries, and other clean energy technologies could also benefit from quantum simulation. These materials must be designed at the atomic level to optimize their electronic and optical properties, requiring understanding of quantum mechanical phenomena that are difficult to model classically. Quantum computers could accelerate materials discovery by enabling more accurate prediction of material properties.

Quantum simulation could also advance understanding of biological processes involved in environmental remediation. Plants and microorganisms use quantum mechanical processes for photosynthesis and other biochemical reactions that could inspire new environmental technologies. Quantum computers could help scientists understand and potentially enhance these natural processes for environmental applications.

Renewable Energy Optimization

The integration of renewable energy sources into electrical grids presents complex optimization challenges that could benefit from quantum computing approaches. Solar and wind power generation varies unpredictably with weather conditions, requiring sophisticated algorithms to balance supply and demand while maintaining grid stability. Current optimization approaches struggle with the scale and complexity of modern electrical grids.

Quantum computers could potentially solve grid optimization problems more efficiently than classical approaches, enabling better integration of renewable energy sources. These optimization problems involve finding optimal solutions across exponentially large solution spaces—exactly the type of problem where quantum computers could provide significant advantages.

Energy storage optimization represents another application where quantum computing could provide benefits. Determining optimal charging and discharging patterns for large arrays of batteries requires solving complex optimization problems that account for electricity prices, demand forecasts, and battery degradation. Quantum algorithms could potentially find better solutions to these problems, improving the economics of renewable energy systems.

The development of smart grid technologies could also benefit from quantum computing approaches. Smart grids require real-time optimization of energy flows across complex networks of generators, storage systems, and consumers. Quantum computers could potentially enable more sophisticated smart grid algorithms that improve efficiency and reliability while reducing costs.

Financial Modeling and Optimization

Portfolio Optimization and Risk Management

The financial services industry faces computational challenges that align remarkably well with quantum computing capabilities. Portfolio optimization—determining the best allocation of investments across thousands of securities to maximize returns while minimizing risk—requires exploring exponentially large solution spaces that challenge classical computers. Current approaches use approximations and heuristics that may miss optimal solutions or fail to account for complex market dynamics.

Quantum computers could revolutionize portfolio optimization by exploring multiple investment scenarios simultaneously through quantum superposition. Quantum algorithms could potentially identify optimal portfolios that classical approaches might never discover, providing competitive advantages to financial institutions that adopt quantum computing early. The financial sector's $ 622 billion quantum market potential by 2035 reflects industry recognition of these opportunities.

Risk management in financial services requires analyzing vast amounts of market data to identify potential threats to investment portfolios. Current risk models struggle to capture complex correlations between different market factors, particularly during periods of market stress when historical relationships break down. Quantum computers could potentially identify subtle patterns in financial data that classical analysis might miss, enabling more robust risk management approaches.

Credit risk assessment presents another application where quantum computing could provide advantages. Determining the likelihood that borrowers will default on loans requires analyzing complex patterns in financial behavior, credit history, and economic conditions. Quantum machine learning algorithms could potentially identify more accurate predictors of credit risk, enabling better lending decisions and reduced loan losses.

High-Frequency Trading and Market Analysis

High-frequency trading firms seek computational advantages that enable them to identify and exploit brief market opportunities before competitors. These firms already invest heavily in cutting-edge classical computing technology, including custom processors, high-speed networks, and advanced algorithms. Quantum computing could provide new sources of competitive advantage in this technology-intensive industry.

Yapı Kredi Bank demonstrated quantum computing's potential for financial analysis by reducing financial crash analysis from years to just 7 seconds using quantum algorithms. This dramatic speedup illustrates how quantum computers could enable financial institutions to respond more quickly to market changes and potential crisis scenarios.

Quantum computers achieve 100 times greater precision in quantum optical atomic clocks compared to classical timing systems, enabling improvements in high-frequency trading systems that depend on precise timing for competitive advantage. These precision improvements could enable new trading strategies that exploit even smaller market inefficiencies.

Market prediction and algorithmic trading could also benefit from quantum machine learning approaches. Financial markets generate enormous amounts of data that contain subtle patterns related to price movements, trading volumes, and market sentiment. Quantum algorithms could potentially identify patterns in this data that classical approaches cannot detect, enabling more profitable trading strategies.

Fraud Detection and Financial Security

Financial fraud detection requires analyzing enormous amounts of transaction data to identify suspicious patterns that might indicate fraudulent activity. Current fraud detection systems use classical machine learning approaches that struggle to identify sophisticated fraud schemes that deliberately avoid detection. Quantum machine learning could potentially identify more subtle indicators of fraudulent behavior.

Yapı Kredi Bank's ability to analyze 600,000+ corporate clients in real-time for systemic risk detection demonstrates quantum computing's potential for large-scale financial analysis. This capability could extend to fraud detection systems that monitor millions of transactions simultaneously for signs of fraudulent activity.

Quantum computing could also enhance financial security through quantum cryptography and quantum key distribution. While quantum computers threaten current encryption methods, they also enable new forms of cryptographic security that are theoretically unbreakable. Financial institutions could use quantum cryptography to protect sensitive financial communications and transactions.

The development of quantum-resistant cryptographic systems represents a crucial application for financial services. As quantum computers become capable of breaking current encryption methods, financial institutions must transition to new cryptographic approaches that remain secure against quantum attacks. Early adoption of quantum-resistant security measures could provide competitive advantages and reduce security risks.

Other Transformative Applications

Artificial Intelligence Acceleration

The intersection of quantum computing and artificial intelligence represents one of the most promising areas for transformative applications. Many AI algorithms involve optimization problems, pattern recognition tasks, and high-dimensional data analysis that align well with quantum computing capabilities. As both technologies mature, their combination could enable AI systems that are dramatically more powerful than classical approaches alone.

Machine learning training often requires optimizing complex mathematical functions across high-dimensional parameter spaces. Current AI training requires massive computational resources and energy consumption, with the largest AI models requiring months of training on supercomputers. Quantum computers could potentially accelerate this training process by exploring parameter spaces more efficiently through quantum superposition and entanglement.

Google's Quantum AI team has demonstrated promising results combining quantum computing with machine learning, using quantum processors to optimize neural network training. Their research suggests that quantum computers could provide exponential speedups for certain machine learning tasks, particularly those involving optimization in high-dimensional spaces.

The development of quantum machine learning algorithms could enable AI systems that can process quantum data directly, rather than requiring classical preprocessing of quantum information. This capability could be particularly valuable for applications involving quantum sensors, quantum communication systems, and quantum simulation data.

Materials Science and Engineering

Quantum computers could revolutionize materials science by enabling accurate simulation of material properties at the atomic level. Current materials research relies heavily on trial-and-error experimentation because classical computers cannot accurately predict how atoms will arrange themselves in new materials or how these arrangements will affect material properties.

The development of superconductors that operate at room temperature represents one of the most sought-after goals in materials science. Room-temperature superconductors could revolutionize electrical grids, transportation systems, and computing technologies by eliminating electrical resistance losses. Quantum computers could potentially accelerate superconductor discovery by simulating the quantum mechanical phenomena that enable superconductivity.

Battery technology development could also benefit significantly from quantum simulation. Next-generation batteries require materials that can store more energy, charge faster, and last longer than current technologies. Understanding how ions move through battery materials and how chemical reactions affect battery performance involves quantum mechanical processes that quantum computers could model more accurately.

The design of catalysts for chemical manufacturing represents another promising application for quantum simulation. Catalysts enable industrial chemical reactions while remaining unchanged themselves, but designing effective catalysts requires understanding quantum mechanical interactions between molecules and catalyst surfaces. Quantum computers could accelerate catalyst discovery, leading to more efficient chemical manufacturing processes.

Logistics and Supply Chain Optimization

Global supply chains involve complex optimization problems that challenge current computational approaches. Companies must coordinate transportation, inventory, manufacturing, and distribution across networks involving thousands of suppliers, millions of products, and constantly changing constraints. Current optimization approaches use approximations that may miss optimal solutions or fail to adapt quickly to changing conditions.

Quantum computers could potentially solve supply chain optimization problems more effectively by exploring vast solution spaces through quantum superposition. These problems often involve finding optimal solutions subject to multiple constraints—exactly the type of problem where quantum algorithms could provide significant advantages over classical approaches.

The COVID-19 pandemic highlighted the fragility of global supply chains and the importance of robust optimization algorithms that can adapt to disruptions. Quantum-enhanced supply chain management could provide more resilient optimization approaches that account for uncertainty and enable rapid adaptation to changing conditions.

Transportation optimization represents a specific area where quantum computing could provide immediate benefits. Routing delivery vehicles, scheduling aircraft, and optimizing shipping routes involve complex optimization problems that affect both costs and environmental impact. Quantum algorithms could potentially find more efficient solutions that reduce both expenses and carbon emissions.

Cybersecurity and Quantum Cryptography

While quantum computers threaten current cryptographic systems, they also enable new forms of cybersecurity that are theoretically unbreakable. Quantum key distribution uses quantum mechanical principles to detect eavesdropping attempts, providing cryptographic security that is guaranteed by the laws of physics rather than computational assumptions.

Quantum random number generation provides another security application for quantum technologies. Many cryptographic systems depend on high-quality random numbers, but classical computers can only generate pseudo-random numbers that may contain subtle patterns. Quantum computers can generate truly random numbers based on quantum mechanical processes, providing enhanced security for cryptographic applications.

The development of quantum-enhanced security protocols could provide new tools for protecting sensitive information in the quantum age. These protocols combine classical cryptographic techniques with quantum mechanical phenomena to create security systems that remain secure even against adversaries with quantum computers.

Quantum sensing applications could also enhance cybersecurity by detecting unauthorized access attempts or tampering with sensitive equipment. Quantum sensors can detect extremely small changes in magnetic fields, electric fields, and other physical parameters that might indicate security breaches.

The promise of quantum computing applications extends across virtually every industry that depends on computational problem-solving. From accelerating scientific discovery to optimizing business operations, quantum computers could provide tools for addressing some of humanity's most pressing challenges. However, realizing this promise requires continued advances in quantum hardware, algorithm development, and the integration of quantum computing with existing technological infrastructure.

Chapter 7: The Threat - Quantum Computing's Dark Side

Every revolutionary technology brings both unprecedented opportunities and serious risks, and quantum computing represents perhaps the most dramatic example of this duality in modern technological development. The same quantum computers that promise to revolutionize drug discovery, optimize supply chains, and accelerate scientific research also pose existential threats to the cryptographic systems that protect our digital civilization. The transition to a quantum-enabled world will require navigating these threats carefully while preserving the security and stability that modern society depends upon.

The quantum threat is not a distant concern for future generations—it represents an immediate challenge that organizations worldwide must address today. While large-scale, fault-tolerant quantum computers capable of breaking current encryption may still be years away, the timeline for quantum threats is compressed by two crucial factors: the long lead times required to upgrade cryptographic infrastructure and the possibility of unexpected breakthroughs that could accelerate quantum computer development beyond current projections.

Understanding quantum computing's threatening capabilities requires examining not just what these machines can do, but when these capabilities might become available and how quickly they could be deployed against existing systems. The asymmetric nature of the quantum threat—where a single sufficiently powerful quantum computer could compromise millions of encrypted systems—means that preparation cannot wait for quantum computers to become reality. The time to prepare for quantum threats is now, while defensive measures can still be implemented before quantum attacks become possible.

The End of Current Cryptography

RSA Encryption Under Siege

The foundation of modern internet security rests on a mathematical assumption that has held true for over four decades: factoring large numbers is computationally intractable for practical purposes. RSA encryption, which protects everything from online banking to private messaging, relies on the difficulty of factoring numbers that are products of two large prime numbers. Current classical computers would require longer than the age of the universe to factor the 2048-bit numbers commonly used in RSA encryption.

Peter Shor's quantum algorithm shatters this assumption completely. A sufficiently powerful quantum computer running Shor's algorithm could factor these supposedly secure numbers in hours or days rather than eons. This capability doesn't just threaten RSA encryption—it undermines the mathematical foundations that make current cryptographic security possible.

The timeline for this cryptographic apocalypse remains uncertain but concerning. Conservative estimates suggest that quantum computers capable of breaking 2048-bit RSA encryption might emerge within 15 to 30 years, while more optimistic projections for quantum hardware development suggest this capability could arrive within 10 to 15 years. However, the possibility of unexpected breakthroughs, such as Microsoft's topological qubit program succeeding or major advances in photonic quantum computing, could compress these timelines dramatically.

The scale of RSA encryption deployment makes this threat particularly serious. Millions of websites use RSA encryption to protect sensitive communications, and countless devices embed RSA keys for secure operation. Upgrading all these systems to quantum-resistant alternatives will require coordinated global effort spanning years or decades. The mismatch between quantum computer development timelines and cryptographic infrastructure upgrade timelines creates a dangerous vulnerability window.

Elliptic Curve Cryptography Vulnerabilities

Elliptic Curve Cryptography (ECC) represents another cornerstone of modern cryptographic security that faces quantum threats. ECC provides equivalent security to RSA using smaller key sizes, making it particularly popular for mobile devices and embedded systems where computational resources are limited. Unfortunately, quantum computers can break ECC even more efficiently than RSA using variations of Shor's algorithm.

The quantum threat to ECC is particularly concerning because of its widespread deployment in constrained environments. Smart cards, mobile phones, Internet of Things devices, and automotive systems commonly use ECC for cryptographic security. These embedded systems often cannot be updated easily, creating long-term vulnerabilities that may persist even after quantum-resistant alternatives become available.

The efficiency of quantum attacks against ECC means that relatively modest quantum computers could break elliptic curve systems before they can break equivalent-strength RSA systems. This timeline compression could create situations where ECC systems become vulnerable to quantum attacks before RSA systems, potentially creating mixed security environments where some systems remain secure while others become compromised.

Digital Certificates and Public Key Infrastructure

The compromise of public key cryptography extends beyond individual encryption systems to threaten the entire public key infrastructure (PKI) that enables secure internet communications. Digital certificates, which establish the authenticity of websites and secure communications, rely on RSA and ECC cryptography for their security. Quantum computers could forge digital certificates, enabling attacks that compromise the entire trust model of internet security.

Certificate authorities—the organizations that issue digital certificates—represent particularly valuable targets for quantum attacks. Compromising a major certificate authority could enable attackers to forge certificates for any website or service, completely undermining secure communications across the internet. The global nature of PKI means that quantum attacks against certificate authorities could have worldwide impact.

The long lifetimes of some digital certificates compound the quantum threat. Certificates issued today with 10-year validity periods could still be in use when quantum computers become capable of breaking their cryptographic protection. This temporal vulnerability means that the quantum threat affects not just future systems, but current cryptographic deployments that may remain in use during the quantum transition.

Cryptocurrency Vulnerabilities

Bitcoin and Blockchain Security

Bitcoin and other cryptocurrencies rely fundamentally on cryptographic security to prevent counterfeiting, ensure transaction integrity, and protect user funds. The cryptographic algorithms that secure blockchain systems—primarily elliptic curve digital signatures and hash functions—face varying degrees of quantum threat that could undermine the entire cryptocurrency ecosystem.

Bitcoin addresses are generated using elliptic curve cryptography, making them vulnerable to quantum attacks using Shor's algorithm. A quantum computer capable of breaking elliptic curve systems could potentially steal bitcoins from any address where funds have been spent, because spending bitcoins reveals the public key associated with that address. This vulnerability affects millions of bitcoin addresses and could compromise a substantial portion of all bitcoins in circulation.

The timeline for quantum threats to Bitcoin creates urgency for cryptocurrency security upgrades. While Bitcoin's cryptographic parameters provide security equivalent to approximately 128-bit symmetric encryption, quantum computers could potentially break these parameters with fewer qubits than required to break 2048-bit RSA systems. This compressed timeline means that Bitcoin may face quantum threats before traditional internet infrastructure.

The decentralized nature of cryptocurrency systems complicates defensive upgrades. Unlike centralized systems where security updates can be deployed rapidly, cryptocurrency networks require consensus among distributed participants to implement security changes. This consensus requirement could slow the deployment of quantum-resistant security measures, creating vulnerabilities during the transition period.

Mining and Consensus Mechanisms

Cryptocurrency mining relies on computational competitions where miners race to solve cryptographic puzzles that secure blockchain networks. Current mining uses SHA-256 hash functions that appear to be less vulnerable to quantum attacks than public key cryptography, but quantum computers could still provide advantages in mining competitions.

Grover's quantum algorithm provides quadratic speedups for searching through large solution spaces, potentially giving quantum-equipped miners advantages over classical mining operations. While this advantage is less dramatic than the exponential speedups that quantum computers provide for factoring, it could still disrupt the economics of cryptocurrency mining and potentially centralize mining power among organizations with access to quantum computers.

The energy consumption associated with cryptocurrency mining represents another area where quantum computers could have significant impact. Current cryptocurrency networks consume enormous amounts of electrical energy for mining operations, contributing to environmental concerns about cryptocurrency adoption. Quantum computers could potentially enable more energy-efficient consensus mechanisms that maintain security while reducing environmental impact.

Proof-of-stake and other alternative consensus mechanisms may be less vulnerable to quantum attacks than proof-of-work mining, but they still rely on cryptographic security that quantum computers could threaten. The transition to quantum-resistant consensus mechanisms will require careful analysis of quantum threats to different blockchain security models.

Digital Asset Protection

The protection of digital assets extends beyond cryptocurrencies to include non-fungible tokens (NFTs), digital contracts, and other blockchain-based assets that depend on cryptographic security. Quantum computers could potentially compromise the authenticity and ownership records of these digital assets, undermining the trust that makes them valuable.

Smart contracts—self-executing contracts with terms directly written into code—often rely on cryptographic security to ensure that contract terms cannot be modified maliciously. Quantum attacks could potentially compromise smart contract security, enabling unauthorized modifications or theft of assets controlled by smart contracts.

The global nature of cryptocurrency markets means that quantum attacks could have immediate worldwide impact. Unlike traditional financial systems that operate within national regulatory frameworks, cryptocurrency networks span international boundaries and could spread quantum attack effects rapidly across global markets.

Digital wallet security represents a particularly vulnerable point in cryptocurrency systems. Most cryptocurrency users store their funds in digital wallets protected by elliptic curve cryptography. Quantum computers capable of breaking these cryptographic protections could potentially steal funds from millions of digital wallets simultaneously, creating catastrophic losses for cryptocurrency users.

National Security Implications

Intelligence and Military Communications

National security agencies and military organizations rely heavily on cryptographic security to protect classified information, secure communications, and maintain operational security. The quantum threat to cryptography poses direct challenges to national security capabilities worldwide, potentially compromising intelligence operations, diplomatic communications, and military coordination.

The long-term value of intelligence information creates particular vulnerabilities to quantum attacks. Adversaries could collect encrypted intelligence communications today with the intention of decrypting them using future quantum computers. This "harvest now, decrypt later" threat means that current intelligence communications could be compromised retroactively when quantum computers become sufficiently powerful.

Military command and control systems depend on secure communications to coordinate operations across global distances. Quantum attacks against military cryptography could compromise operational security, endanger personnel, and undermine military effectiveness. The high stakes of military operations make even brief cryptographic vulnerabilities potentially catastrophic.

Satellite communications represent another vulnerable area where quantum attacks could have strategic implications. Many civilian and military satellite systems use cryptographic security that quantum computers could compromise, potentially disrupting communications, navigation, and reconnaissance capabilities that modern military operations depend upon.

Critical Infrastructure Protection

Power grids, transportation systems, water treatment facilities, and other critical infrastructure increasingly depend on digital control systems that use cryptographic security. Quantum attacks against these systems could enable adversaries to disrupt essential services, cause economic damage, or threaten public safety.

The industrial control systems that manage critical infrastructure often use cryptographic protocols that were designed when quantum threats seemed distant and theoretical. Many of these systems have long operational lifetimes and cannot be upgraded easily, creating persistent vulnerabilities that may extend well into the quantum era.

The interconnected nature of modern infrastructure means that quantum attacks against one system could cascade into broader failures. Disrupting electrical grid communications could affect transportation systems, water treatment facilities, and telecommunications networks that depend on reliable electrical power. These cascading effects could amplify the impact of quantum attacks beyond their immediate targets.

Economic Espionage and Intellectual Property

Quantum computers could enable new forms of economic espionage that threaten intellectual property, trade secrets, and competitive information. Companies rely on cryptographic security to protect proprietary information, research data, and strategic plans. Quantum attacks could compromise this protection, enabling competitors or foreign adversaries to steal valuable intellectual property.

The global nature of modern business means that quantum attacks could have immediate international impact. Multinational corporations routinely transmit sensitive information across international boundaries using cryptographic protection that quantum computers could compromise. These attacks could affect trade relationships, competitive positions, and economic stability.

Research and development information represents particularly valuable targets for quantum-enabled economic espionage. Understanding competitors' research directions, product development plans, and technological capabilities could provide substantial economic advantages to organizations with quantum attack capabilities.

The timeline compression created by quantum threats means that organizations must begin protecting sensitive information against future quantum attacks today. Information that seems adequately protected by current cryptographic standards may become vulnerable when quantum computers mature, requiring proactive security measures that account for future quantum capabilities.

The dark side of quantum computing creates unprecedented challenges for maintaining security and stability in an increasingly digital world. The threats posed by quantum computers are not speculative future concerns—they represent immediate challenges that require coordinated responses from governments, corporations, and international organizations. The race to develop quantum computers capable of breaking current security systems is matched by equally urgent efforts to develop defensive technologies that can preserve security in the quantum age.

Understanding these threats is essential for preparing for the quantum future, but it's equally important to recognize that quantum computing also provides tools for addressing the very security challenges it creates. The next chapter will examine how organizations worldwide are developing quantum-resistant security measures and preparing for the transition to post-quantum cryptography, ensuring that the quantum revolution enhances rather than undermines our technological civilization.

Chapter 8: The Response - Preparing for a Quantum World

The quantum threat to cryptographic security has prompted the most comprehensive overhaul of digital security infrastructure in the history of computing. Unlike previous security challenges that affected specific systems or applications, the quantum threat requires fundamental changes to the cryptographic foundations that protect virtually every aspect of our digital civilization. This transition represents one of the largest coordinated technology upgrades ever attempted, involving governments, corporations, and international organizations working together to deploy quantum-resistant security measures before quantum computers become capable of breaking current systems.

The urgency of this transition cannot be overstated. While quantum computers capable of breaking current encryption may still be years away, the long lead times required for security upgrades mean that preparation must begin immediately. Large organizations may require five to ten years to identify all cryptographic dependencies, test quantum-resistant alternatives, and deploy upgraded systems across their entire infrastructure. The window for proactive preparation is narrow and closing rapidly as quantum computer capabilities continue to advance.

The response to quantum threats involves three critical components: developing new cryptographic methods that remain secure against quantum attacks, upgrading existing infrastructure to use quantum-resistant security measures, and creating policy frameworks that guide the quantum transition while addressing its broader implications for society. Each component presents unique challenges that require coordinated solutions spanning technical, economic, and regulatory domains.

Post-Quantum Cryptography

The Search for Quantum-Resistant Algorithms

The development of post-quantum cryptography represents one of the most intensive cryptographic research efforts in history. Unlike previous cryptographic advances that typically involved incremental improvements to existing methods, post-quantum cryptography requires entirely new mathematical foundations that can withstand attacks from both classical and quantum computers. The National Institute of Standards and Technology (NIST) has led a global effort to identify, evaluate, and standardize these new cryptographic approaches.

The NIST Post-Quantum Cryptography Standardization process began in 2016 with 82 candidate algorithms submitted by researchers worldwide. Through multiple rounds of evaluation involving security analysis, performance testing, and implementation studies, NIST narrowed this field to a small number of algorithms suitable for standardization. In 2024, NIST published the first post-quantum cryptographic standards, marking a crucial milestone in the transition to quantum-resistant security.

The selected algorithms rely on mathematical problems that appear difficult for both classical and quantum computers to solve. These include lattice-based cryptography that depends on finding short vectors in high-dimensional lattices, code-based cryptography that relies on decoding random linear codes, and hash-based signature schemes that depend only on the security of cryptographic hash functions. Each approach offers different trade-offs between security, performance, and implementation complexity.

However, post-quantum cryptography faces significant deployment challenges. The new algorithms typically require larger key sizes, consume more computational resources, and produce longer signatures than current cryptographic methods. These increased requirements affect everything from network bandwidth to battery life in mobile devices, requiring careful optimization to maintain acceptable performance while providing quantum-resistant security.

Implementation Challenges and Solutions

Deploying post-quantum cryptography across existing infrastructure requires addressing numerous practical challenges that extend beyond simply replacing one algorithm with another. Current systems embed cryptographic assumptions throughout their design, from the sizes of data structures that store cryptographic keys to the network protocols that exchange cryptographic information. Upgrading to post-quantum cryptography may require fundamental changes to system architectures.

The increased computational requirements of post-quantum algorithms particularly affect resource-constrained devices like Internet of Things sensors, smart cards, and embedded systems. These devices often lack the processing power and memory needed for the larger key sizes and more complex operations required by quantum-resistant algorithms. Specialized implementations optimized for constrained environments represent an active area of research and development.

Hybrid security approaches that combine classical and post-quantum cryptographic methods provide one strategy for managing the transition to quantum-resistant security. These hybrid systems use both current and quantum-resistant algorithms simultaneously, providing protection against both classical and quantum attacks while enabling gradual migration as post-quantum implementations mature and improve.

The backwards compatibility requirements for post-quantum cryptography create additional complexity. Systems must often support both current and quantum-resistant algorithms during transition periods, enabling secure communication between upgraded and legacy systems. This dual-algorithm support increases implementation complexity while providing flexibility for gradual migration approaches.

Testing and Validation

The deployment of post-quantum cryptography requires extensive testing and validation to ensure that new algorithms provide the expected security benefits without introducing unexpected vulnerabilities. Unlike classical cryptographic algorithms that have been analyzed for decades, post-quantum algorithms are relatively new and may contain subtle weaknesses that researchers haven't yet discovered.

The mathematical foundations of post-quantum cryptography differ significantly from current algorithms, requiring new analysis techniques and security models. Researchers must evaluate not just the theoretical security of these algorithms, but also their resistance to implementation attacks that exploit physical properties of computing systems rather than mathematical weaknesses.

Side-channel attacks represent a particular concern for post-quantum cryptography implementation. These attacks exploit information leaked through power consumption, electromagnetic radiation, or timing variations during cryptographic operations. Post-quantum algorithms may be vulnerable to different types of side-channel attacks than current algorithms, requiring new countermeasures and protection techniques.

The validation process for post-quantum cryptography also involves testing interoperability between different implementations and ensuring that new algorithms integrate properly with existing security protocols. This testing requires coordination between algorithm developers, software vendors, and system integrators to identify and resolve compatibility issues before widespread deployment.

Quantum-Safe Infrastructure

Enterprise Migration Strategies

Large organizations face the daunting task of upgrading massive technology infrastructures to use quantum-resistant security measures while maintaining business continuity and acceptable performance. Enterprise migration to post-quantum cryptography requires systematic identification of all cryptographic dependencies, careful planning of upgrade sequences, and extensive testing to ensure that new security measures work correctly in complex production environments.

The first step in enterprise quantum-safe migration involves conducting comprehensive cryptographic inventories to identify every system, application, and device that uses cryptographic security. This discovery process often reveals cryptographic dependencies that organizations didn't know existed, from embedded certificates in legacy systems to cryptographic libraries used by third-party software components.

Risk assessment and prioritization represent crucial aspects of enterprise migration planning. Organizations must identify which systems face the greatest quantum threats and which systems are most critical to business operations. High-value targets like financial systems, customer databases, and intellectual property repositories may require immediate attention, while less sensitive systems might be upgraded during routine maintenance cycles.

The migration process itself requires careful orchestration to avoid security vulnerabilities during the transition period. Organizations must ensure that upgraded systems can communicate securely with legacy systems while gradually expanding quantum-resistant security coverage across their entire infrastructure. This process may require years of careful planning and execution for large organizations with complex technology environments.

Cloud and Infrastructure Providers

Cloud computing providers play a crucial role in the quantum-safe transition because they provide computing and networking services to millions of customers worldwide. These providers must upgrade their infrastructure to support post-quantum cryptography while ensuring that customer applications continue to work correctly with new security measures.

Amazon, Microsoft, Google, and other major cloud providers have announced roadmaps for deploying post-quantum cryptography across their services. These upgrades affect everything from data encryption and network communications to identity authentication and digital certificates. The scale of these upgrades—affecting millions of servers and network devices—represents one of the largest coordinated security upgrades ever attempted.

The cloud providers' approach to quantum-safe migration often involves offering multiple cryptographic options that customers can choose based on their specific security requirements and performance constraints. This flexibility enables gradual migration while accommodating different customer needs and timeline constraints.

Networking infrastructure providers face similar challenges in upgrading the core internet infrastructure to support post-quantum cryptography. Internet backbone providers, content delivery networks, and telecommunications companies must coordinate upgrades to ensure continued secure communications across global networks during the quantum transition.

IoT and Embedded Systems

Internet of Things devices and embedded systems present some of the most challenging aspects of the quantum-safe transition. These systems often operate for decades with minimal maintenance, use resource-constrained processors with limited computational capabilities, and may lack update mechanisms that enable remote security upgrades.

The longevity of embedded systems means that devices deployed today may still be operating when quantum computers become capable of breaking their current security measures. Automotive systems, industrial control equipment, and infrastructure monitoring devices often operate for 10 to 20 years or longer, spanning the entire timeline during which quantum threats are expected to emerge.

Resource constraints in IoT devices limit the post-quantum cryptographic algorithms that can be implemented effectively. These devices often have limited memory, processing power, and battery life that cannot support the increased computational requirements of many quantum-resistant algorithms. Specialized post-quantum algorithms optimized for constrained environments represent an active area of research and development.

The update mechanisms for IoT and embedded systems vary widely, with some devices supporting over-the-air updates while others require physical access for security upgrades. This variability complicates the deployment of quantum-resistant security measures and may require replacement of devices that cannot be upgraded remotely.

Policy and Regulatory Challenges

International Coordination and Standards

The global nature of quantum threats requires unprecedented international cooperation to ensure that quantum-resistant security measures work effectively across national boundaries and different regulatory frameworks. Cryptographic standards must be compatible worldwide to enable secure international communications and commerce during the quantum transition.

International standardization organizations including NIST, the International Organization for Standardization (ISO), and the Internet Engineering Task Force (IETF) are working to ensure that post-quantum cryptographic standards are compatible across different countries and regions. This coordination process involves balancing security requirements with practical implementation constraints while accommodating different national security concerns and regulatory approaches.

The quantum transition also requires coordination of timeline and migration strategies to avoid creating security vulnerabilities at the interfaces between different systems and countries. If some regions upgrade to post-quantum cryptography much faster than others, the resulting incompatibilities could disrupt international communications and commerce.

Export controls and technology transfer restrictions complicate international cooperation in quantum technology development. While cooperation is essential for addressing quantum threats, countries also compete for quantum technology advantages, creating tensions between openness and security that affect international quantum research collaboration.

Regulatory Frameworks and Compliance

Government regulatory agencies are developing new frameworks for managing quantum technology risks while enabling beneficial quantum applications. These frameworks must balance the need to prepare for quantum threats with the desire to foster quantum technology innovation and economic development.

Financial services regulations are evolving to address quantum threats to banking and financial infrastructure. Regulatory agencies are beginning to require financial institutions to assess their quantum risk exposure and develop plans for transitioning to quantum-resistant security measures. These requirements recognize the critical importance of financial system security and the potentially devastating impact of quantum attacks on financial infrastructure.

Healthcare regulations must also adapt to address quantum threats to medical information security and the opportunities that quantum computing provides for medical research and patient care. The protection of sensitive medical information requires robust security measures that remain effective against quantum attacks, while quantum computing applications in drug discovery and medical research require regulatory frameworks that enable innovation while protecting patient safety.

Critical infrastructure regulations are being updated to address quantum threats to power grids, transportation systems, and communications networks. These systems represent particularly attractive targets for quantum attacks because of their essential role in supporting modern society and their often extensive use of cryptographic security for operational control.

Workforce Development and Education

The quantum transition requires developing a workforce with expertise in both quantum technologies and quantum-resistant security measures. This workforce development challenge spans multiple educational levels, from training current professionals in quantum-safe security practices to educating the next generation of quantum researchers and engineers.

Universities are rapidly expanding quantum computing and quantum information science programs to meet growing demand for quantum-educated professionals. These programs must balance theoretical quantum mechanics education with practical skills in quantum programming, quantum algorithm development, and quantum security implementation. The interdisciplinary nature of quantum technology requires educational approaches that span physics, computer science, mathematics, and engineering.

Professional development programs are helping current technology workers develop quantum literacy without requiring complete career changes. Cybersecurity professionals need training in post-quantum cryptography implementation, software developers need quantum programming skills, and system administrators need understanding of quantum safe infrastructure management.

The global competition for quantum talent has created talent shortage concerns in countries that are investing heavily in quantum technology development. Addressing these shortages requires both expanding domestic quantum education programs and attracting international talent through immigration and collaboration policies that balance openness with security concerns.

Economic and Societal Implications

The transition to quantum-safe infrastructure involves substantial economic costs that must be balanced against the risks of quantum attacks. Organizations must invest in new security technologies, upgrade existing systems, and retrain personnel, while the benefits of these investments may not become apparent until quantum threats materialize. This temporal mismatch between costs and benefits creates challenges for justifying quantum-safe investments.

The societal implications of the quantum transition extend beyond technology and economics to affect privacy, civil liberties, and international relations. Quantum technologies could enable new forms of surveillance and monitoring that challenge traditional privacy expectations, while quantum communication technologies could provide enhanced privacy protections that are theoretically unbreakable.

The uneven global development of quantum technologies could create new forms of technological inequality between countries and regions with different levels of quantum capability. Nations that achieve quantum advantages first may gain significant economic and security benefits, while those that lag behind could face disadvantages in international competition and cooperation.

Chapter 9: The Future - Life in the Quantum Age

As we stand on the threshold of the quantum age, we can glimpse a future that seems simultaneously familiar and utterly transformed. The quantum revolution will not replace our digital world overnight—instead, it will enhance and extend our technological capabilities in ways that fundamentally change what becomes possible. From revolutionizing scientific discovery to enabling new forms of artificial intelligence, quantum computing will create opportunities that are difficult to imagine from our current technological perspective.

The timeline for quantum computing's transformation of society is compressed compared to previous technological revolutions. While the transition from mechanical to electronic computers took decades, quantum computing's impact will likely unfold more rapidly due to the mature software development capabilities, global communication networks, and established technology adoption patterns that didn't exist during earlier computing transitions. Industry analysis for 2025 shows quantum computing revenue exceeding 1billion,upfrom1*billion,upfrom* 650 to 750 million in 2024, reflecting accelerating commercial adoption of quantum technologies.

The future quantum landscape will be shaped by the convergence of multiple technological trends that are already visible today. Improved logical qubits, specialized quantum hardware and software, networked quantum systems, enhanced software abstraction layers, expanded workforce development programs, and continued advances in physical qubit implementations represent the six most important trends driving quantum computing development. Understanding how these trends will evolve and interact provides insights into the quantum future that awaits us.

Timeline for Practical Quantum Computing

Near-Term Quantum Applications (2025-2030)

The immediate future of quantum computing will be characterized by specialized applications that leverage current noisy intermediate-scale quantum (NISQ) capabilities while providing genuine business value despite their limitations. The financial services industry is anticipated to become one of the earliest adopters of commercially useful quantum computing technologies, with applications in portfolio optimization, risk analysis, and fraud detection becoming available within the next few years.

IBM's quantum-centric supercomputer targets of over 4,000 qubits by 2025 represent ambitious but achievable goals that could enable the first practical quantum advantages for optimization and simulation problems. These systems will use modular architectures like the IBM Quantum System Two, supporting up to 16,632 qubits through networking multiple quantum processors together. The focus on improving circuit quality to run 5,000 gates with parametric circuits demonstrates progress toward quantum systems capable of solving real-world problems.

Google's roadmap aims for useful, error-corrected quantum computers by 2029, building on their quantum supremacy demonstrations and progress toward logical qubits. CEO Sundar Pichai has emphasized quantum computing's potential role in addressing global challenges like climate change and drug discovery, predicting transformative impacts between 2025 and 2030. Recent progress with their Willow chip shows error reduction through increased physical qubit resources, validating their approach to fault-tolerant quantum computing.

The Development Advanced Research Projects Agency (DARPA) US2QC program is investigating whether quantum computing approaches can achieve utility scale operation—where computational value exceeds cost—by 2033. This program includes Microsoft's topological qubit research and photonic quantum computing approaches, representing government recognition that multiple quantum technologies could achieve practical advantages within this timeframe.

Medium-Term Breakthrough Period (2030-2040)

The 2030s will likely witness the transition from NISQ devices to fault-tolerant quantum computers capable of running complex quantum algorithms without the error limitations that constrain current systems. Microsoft's topological qubit program, if successful, could provide natural error resistance that eliminates cryogenic requirements and provides coherence times 10,000 times longer than current systems. Room-temperature topological qubits would make million-qubit systems suddenly feasible, dramatically accelerating quantum computing adoption.

Photonic quantum computing could provide alternative breakthrough pathways during this period. PsiQuantum's pursuit of million-qubit photonic processors using standard silicon photonics manufacturing could transform quantum computing accessibility. Photonic systems operate at room temperature and can be networked using existing fiber optic infrastructure, potentially making quantum computing as accessible as classical cloud computing.

The algorithmic revolution during this period could prove as important as hardware advances. Building on recent theoretical work showing exponential quantum speedups for certain problem classes, researchers might discover quantum algorithms with broader applicability. The history of classical computing demonstrates that algorithmic breakthroughs often provide larger performance gains than hardware improvements alone.

AI-quantum synergy represents another transformative trend for the 2030s. Artificial intelligence systems might design quantum circuits that humans cannot conceive, discovering non-intuitive approaches to quantum computation. Conversely, quantum processors might provide exponential speedups for certain AI training tasks, creating positive feedback loops where each technology accelerates the other's development.

Long-Term Quantum Integration (2040-2050)

By the 2040s, quantum computing could become fully integrated into the technological infrastructure that supports modern society. Quantum processors might become standard components in data centers, providing specialized computational capabilities alongside classical processors. The distinction between quantum and classical computing may blur as hybrid systems seamlessly combine both approaches to solve complex problems.

The development of quantum internet infrastructure could enable distributed quantum applications that span global distances. Quantum communication networks would provide theoretically unbreakable security for sensitive communications while enabling distributed quantum computing applications that coordinate quantum processors worldwide. This infrastructure could support new forms of digital interaction that are impossible with classical systems alone.

Quantum sensing and metrology applications could achieve precision levels that enable entirely new categories of scientific measurement and technological capability. Quantum sensors could detect gravitational waves with unprecedented sensitivity, measure magnetic fields with atomic-scale resolution, and provide timing precision that enables new navigation and positioning technologies.

The educational system will adapt to include quantum literacy as a fundamental component of technical education. Just as programming skills became essential for many careers during the classical computing revolution, understanding quantum principles and quantum algorithm development may become necessary for careers in science, engineering, and technology.

Societal Transformations Ahead

Healthcare Revolution

The application of quantum computing to healthcare could fundamentally transform medical research, diagnosis, and treatment approaches. Quantum-enhanced drug discovery will accelerate the development of new medications by enabling accurate simulation of molecular interactions that govern drug effectiveness and safety. Pharmaceutical companies could test thousands of potential drug candidates virtually before synthesizing and testing them in laboratories, potentially reducing the time and cost required to bring new treatments to patients.

Personalized medicine will benefit enormously from quantum computing's ability to analyze complex genetic and molecular data. Quantum computers could identify subtle patterns in genomic data that predict individual responses to specific treatments, enabling precision medicine approaches that optimize therapy for each patient's unique biological characteristics. This capability could improve treatment outcomes while reducing adverse reactions and unnecessary medical interventions.

Medical imaging and diagnostic applications could achieve unprecedented accuracy through quantum-enhanced pattern recognition. Quantum machine learning algorithms might identify disease indicators in medical images that human doctors and classical AI systems cannot detect, enabling earlier diagnosis and more effective treatments. Quantum sensors could provide new medical imaging modalities that reveal biological processes at molecular scales.

The development of quantum biosensors could enable real-time monitoring of biological processes that are currently impossible to observe. These sensors could track drug metabolism, monitor immune system responses, and detect early signs of disease progression with sensitivity levels that exceed current medical instrumentation. This monitoring capability could enable proactive healthcare approaches that prevent disease rather than simply treating symptoms.

Financial System Evolution

The financial services industry will undergo fundamental changes as quantum computing capabilities mature and quantum threats to current security systems emerge. The industry's early adoption of quantum technologies for optimization and risk analysis will evolve into comprehensive quantum-enhanced financial systems that provide new capabilities while maintaining security against quantum attacks.

Real-time global risk assessment will become possible through quantum computers' ability to analyze vast datasets and identify subtle correlations that classical systems cannot detect. Financial institutions could monitor systemic risks across global markets simultaneously, potentially preventing financial crises by identifying dangerous accumulations of risk before they become critical.

Algorithmic trading will be transformed by quantum computers' ability to identify patterns in market data and optimize trading strategies across exponentially large parameter spaces. Quantum-enhanced trading systems could provide competitive advantages to financial institutions that adopt quantum technologies early, while quantum-resistant security measures will be essential for protecting these systems against quantum attacks.

Central bank digital currencies (CBDCs) could leverage quantum technologies for both enhanced security and improved functionality. Quantum cryptography could provide theoretically unbreakable security for digital currency transactions, while quantum computing could enable more sophisticated monetary policy implementations that respond dynamically to economic conditions.

Scientific Discovery Acceleration

Quantum computing will accelerate scientific discovery across multiple disciplines by enabling simulation and analysis capabilities that are impossible with classical computers. Climate science will benefit from quantum computers' ability to model atmospheric and oceanic processes at molecular scales, potentially improving weather prediction accuracy and climate change projections.

Materials science research will be revolutionized by quantum computers' ability to predict material properties before synthesis and testing. Researchers could design new materials with precisely specified characteristics for applications ranging from renewable energy to electronics. This capability could accelerate the development of more efficient solar cells, better batteries, and superconductors that operate at practical temperatures.

Fundamental physics research will benefit from quantum computers' natural ability to simulate quantum systems. Researchers could use quantum computers to explore theoretical physics questions that are impossible to investigate experimentally, potentially leading to discoveries about the fundamental nature of space, time, and matter. Quantum computers might even help us understand quantum mechanics itself more deeply.

The acceleration of scientific discovery could create positive feedback loops where quantum-enhanced research leads to better quantum technologies, which enable even more advanced research capabilities. This cycle could drive rapid advances across multiple scientific disciplines simultaneously.

Educational and Workforce Transformation

The quantum age will require fundamental changes to educational systems to prepare students for careers that don't exist today while ensuring that the general population understands quantum technology's implications for society. Quantum literacy will become as important as computer literacy was during the classical computing revolution.

Primary and secondary education will need to incorporate quantum concepts alongside traditional physics and mathematics curricula. Students will need to understand quantum mechanical principles not as abstract theoretical concepts, but as practical foundations for technologies they'll use throughout their careers. This education must balance scientific accuracy with accessibility for students without advanced mathematical backgrounds.

Higher education will expand quantum computing and quantum information science programs to meet growing demand for quantum-educated professionals. These programs must be inherently interdisciplinary, combining physics, computer science, mathematics, and engineering to prepare students for quantum technology careers that span multiple traditional academic boundaries.

Professional development and continuing education programs will help current workers adapt to quantum technology adoption in their industries. Just as the internet revolution required workers to develop new skills while continuing their careers, the quantum revolution will require ongoing learning and adaptation as quantum technologies reshape existing job functions and create entirely new career categories.

Preparing for the Quantum Workforce

New Quantum Career Categories

The quantum revolution will create entirely new categories of employment that combine quantum technology expertise with applications in specific industries. Quantum software engineers will develop applications that leverage quantum computing capabilities while integrating seamlessly with classical computing infrastructure. These professionals will need skills that span quantum algorithm development, classical software engineering, and domain expertise in specific application areas.

Quantum security specialists will become essential for organizations preparing for quantum threats and opportunities. These professionals will need deep understanding of both post-quantum cryptography and quantum technologies to design security systems that remain effective throughout the quantum transition. The critical importance of security during this transition period will create high demand for professionals with these specialized skills.

Quantum system administrators will manage hybrid classical-quantum computing infrastructure as quantum computers become standard components in data centers and cloud computing platforms. These professionals will need operational expertise in quantum hardware maintenance, quantum error correction, and the integration of quantum and classical computing resources.

Quantum application specialists will work in specific industries to identify and implement quantum computing applications that provide business value. These professionals will need both quantum technology expertise and deep knowledge of their specific industry domains, enabling them to translate quantum capabilities into practical business solutions.

Skills for the Quantum Economy

The quantum economy will require workers with hybrid skill sets that combine quantum technology knowledge with expertise in specific application domains. Quantum chemistry researchers will apply quantum computing to molecular simulation and drug discovery. Quantum finance specialists will develop quantum algorithms for optimization and risk analysis. Quantum AI researchers will explore the convergence of quantum computing and artificial intelligence.

Programming skills for the quantum age will involve multiple paradigms. Quantum programmers will need to understand quantum algorithm design principles while also developing classical software that coordinates quantum and classical processing. The probabilistic nature of quantum computation will require new approaches to software testing, debugging, and quality assurance.

Mathematical and statistical skills will become increasingly important as quantum technologies proliferate. Understanding probability theory, linear algebra, and optimization methods will be essential for workers who need to understand quantum algorithm behavior and interpret quantum computing results. These mathematical skills must be combined with practical programming abilities and domain-specific knowledge.

Critical thinking skills for evaluating quantum technology claims will become essential across many industries. As quantum computing hype continues to generate exaggerated claims about quantum capabilities, workers will need the ability to distinguish between genuine quantum advantages and marketing hyperbole. This evaluation capability will be crucial for making informed decisions about quantum technology adoption and investment.

Adapting Existing Industries

Industries across the economy will need to adapt their workforces to incorporate quantum technologies while maintaining competitiveness during the quantum transition. Pharmaceutical companies will train chemists and biologists in quantum simulation techniques. Financial institutions will educate analysts and traders in quantum-enhanced modeling approaches. Manufacturing companies will prepare engineers for quantum-optimized production planning and quality control.

The adaptation process will require careful change management to ensure that organizations can adopt quantum technologies without disrupting existing operations. This transition may involve gradual skill development programs, partnerships with quantum computing companies, and hybrid approaches that combine classical and quantum capabilities while workers develop quantum expertise.

Professional certification and training programs will emerge to help workers develop quantum skills while maintaining their current career trajectories. These programs will need to be accessible to working professionals who cannot return to school full-time while providing rigorous training in quantum technologies and applications.

Industry associations and professional organizations will play crucial roles in developing standards for quantum education and professional development. These organizations will need to establish certification requirements, develop curriculum standards, and coordinate training programs that ensure consistent quality across different educational providers.

The future quantum landscape will be shaped by the choices we make today about education, infrastructure, and technology development. The organizations and individuals who prepare effectively for the quantum age will be positioned to capture the extraordinary opportunities that quantum technologies provide, while those who delay preparation may find themselves disadvantaged in an increasingly quantum-enabled world.

The quantum revolution represents both the greatest technological opportunity and the most significant security challenge of our time. Success in navigating this transition will require coordinated efforts across governments, corporations, educational institutions, and individuals. The future belongs to those who can harness quantum computing's transformative power while managing its disruptive effects on existing technological and social systems.

As we conclude our exploration of the quantum revolution, the most important lesson is that this transformation is already underway. The decisions made today about quantum technology development, security preparation, and workforce development will determine how successfully our society adapts to the quantum age. The quantum future is not something that will happen to us—it is something we are actively creating through our choices and actions today.

Epilogue: The Quantum Paradigm Shift

As we reach the end of our journey through the quantum revolution, it's worth reflecting on the magnitude of the transformation we are witnessing. Standing at this pivotal moment in technological history, we can see both where we've come from and where we're heading. The quantum computing revolution represents more than just another advance in computational power—it embodies a fundamental shift in how we understand and harness the physical world for information processing.

The story we've traced throughout this book—from Max Planck's quantum theory in 1900 to today's quantum-centric supercomputers—reveals a pattern that characterizes all truly transformative technologies. Initially dismissed as academic curiosities with no practical applications, quantum mechanical phenomena gradually revealed their potential for solving problems that seemed permanently beyond reach. Today, as over 100 quantum computing systems operate worldwide and governments pledge $ 40 billion in quantum research investments over the next decade, we stand at the threshold of quantum technology's transition from experimental curiosity to transformative force.

Lessons from Technological Paradigm Shifts

History teaches us valuable lessons about how paradigm shifts unfold and how societies adapt to revolutionary technologies. The transition from mechanical calculation to electronic computation in the mid-20th century offers instructive parallels to today's quantum revolution. Like quantum computers today, early electronic computers were expensive, unreliable, and required specialized expertise to operate. Critics questioned whether these machines would ever become practical for widespread use.

Yet within decades, electronic computers transformed virtually every aspect of human activity. The key insight from this historical precedent is that transformative technologies often exceed even optimistic projections once they achieve critical mass. The internet, originally designed to connect a few dozen research institutions, evolved into the global information infrastructure that now connects billions of people. Similarly, quantum computing may ultimately enable applications that we cannot yet imagine.

The quantum paradigm shift differs from previous technological transitions in crucial ways. Where earlier computing revolutions primarily involved engineering improvements—faster processors, more memory, better software—quantum computing represents a fundamentally different approach to computation itself. Quantum computers don't simply calculate faster; they explore solution spaces using quantum mechanical phenomena that have no classical analogs.

This fundamental difference explains both the extraordinary potential of quantum computing and the challenges we face in realizing that potential. Classical computers became useful through incremental improvements that accumulated over decades. Quantum computers require overcoming threshold effects—critical points where quantum error correction becomes effective, where quantum algorithms provide clear advantages over classical approaches, and where quantum hardware becomes sufficiently reliable for practical applications.

The Current Inflection Point

As we've seen throughout this book, quantum computing in 2025 exists at a unique inflection point. Current quantum computers demonstrate genuine quantum phenomena and can solve certain problems exponentially faster than classical systems, yet they remain too limited and error-prone for most practical applications. This NISQ era represents a transitional phase that is both frustrating and full of promise.

The six key trends shaping quantum computing development in 2025—experiments with logical qubits, specialized hardware and software development, networking of NISQ devices, software abstraction layers, workforce development, and improved physical qubits—all point toward the gradual maturation of quantum technologies. Each trend represents progress toward overcoming the fundamental challenges that currently limit quantum computing applications.

The financial industry's emergence as an early adopter of quantum technologies illustrates how the quantum transition will likely unfold. Rather than sudden replacement of classical systems, we're witnessing gradual integration of quantum capabilities into existing technological infrastructure. Companies are investing in quantum research, training quantum-literate workforces, and preparing for quantum threats to cryptographic security while quantum computers remain experimental technologies.

This preparation reflects hard-won wisdom from previous technological transitions. Organizations that waited too long to adopt personal computers, the internet, or mobile technologies found themselves disadvantaged compared to early adopters. The quantum transition will likely reward organizations that begin preparation now, even though practical quantum advantages may still be years away.

Convergence and Acceleration

One of the most striking aspects of the current quantum moment is the convergence of multiple technological trends that are accelerating quantum development. Advances in artificial intelligence are enabling better quantum error correction, quantum circuit optimization, and quantum algorithm discovery. Meanwhile, quantum computers could provide exponential speedups for certain AI training tasks, creating positive feedback loops where each technology accelerates the other's progress.

The integration of quantum technologies with cloud computing infrastructure is democratizing access to quantum research and development. Where quantum computers once required specialized laboratories with dilution refrigerators and expert operators, cloud-based quantum services now enable anyone with internet access to experiment with quantum algorithms and applications. This accessibility is accelerating innovation by enabling a global community of quantum researchers and developers.

Materials science advances are simultaneously improving quantum hardware capabilities and benefiting from quantum simulation. Better superconducting materials enable longer coherence times for superconducting qubits, while quantum computers help design new materials with precisely specified properties. This reciprocal relationship between quantum computing and materials science exemplifies how quantum technologies will both drive and benefit from advances across multiple scientific disciplines.

The growing investment in quantum technologies—over 2billioninprivatequantumstartupsin2022alone,withprojectionsof2*billioninprivatequantumstartupsin*2022*alone,withprojectionsof* 2 trillion in economic impact by 2035—creates the financial resources needed for rapid scaling of quantum research and development. This investment level approaches the scale of funding that supported the Manhattan Project and the Apollo program, historical examples of sustained technological development programs that achieved seemingly impossible goals through coordinated effort and substantial resources.

Managing the Quantum Transition

The quantum revolution will create both extraordinary opportunities and significant challenges that will require careful management to ensure beneficial outcomes. The threat to current cryptographic systems represents the most immediate challenge, requiring coordinated global effort to upgrade security infrastructure before quantum computers become capable of breaking current encryption methods.

This cryptographic transition illustrates both the challenges and the collaborative potential of the quantum age. Unlike previous security upgrades that affected individual organizations or systems, the quantum threat requires coordinated action across governments, corporations, and international organizations. The successful development and deployment of post-quantum cryptography will demonstrate humanity's ability to address technological challenges through international cooperation and coordinated planning.

The economic implications of quantum computing will likely create both opportunities and inequalities that societies will need to address thoughtfully. Organizations and nations that achieve quantum advantages first may gain significant competitive benefits, while those that lag behind could face technological disadvantages. Managing this transition will require policies that foster quantum innovation while ensuring broad access to quantum benefits.

The workforce development challenges associated with quantum technologies represent another area requiring proactive management. The quantum economy will create entirely new categories of employment while transforming existing jobs across multiple industries. Educational systems must adapt to provide quantum literacy alongside traditional technical skills, while organizations must invest in retraining current workers for quantum-enhanced roles.

The Broader Implications

The quantum revolution extends far beyond computing to encompass quantum sensing, quantum communication, and quantum simulation technologies that will transform multiple aspects of human activity. Quantum sensors could enable detection of gravitational waves with unprecedented sensitivity, measurement of magnetic fields at atomic scales, and timing precision that revolutionizes navigation and positioning technologies.

Quantum communication networks will provide theoretically unbreakable security for sensitive communications while enabling distributed quantum computing applications that coordinate quantum processors across global distances. This quantum internet could support new forms of digital interaction that are impossible with classical systems alone, potentially transforming how we share information and coordinate activities.

The convergence of quantum technologies with biotechnology could accelerate our understanding of biological processes and enable new approaches to medicine and healthcare. Quantum sensors could monitor biological processes at molecular scales, while quantum computers could simulate complex biological systems that remain intractable for classical analysis.

These broader applications of quantum technologies suggest that the quantum revolution will ultimately affect virtually every aspect of human activity, from scientific research and medical treatment to communication and transportation. The societies that successfully navigate this transition will be positioned to capture extraordinary benefits, while those that struggle with quantum adoption may find themselves disadvantaged in an increasingly quantum-enabled world.

Looking Forward

As we look toward the quantum future, several scenarios seem plausible based on current technological trajectories and investment patterns. The most likely scenario involves gradual quantum integration, where quantum technologies slowly augment classical systems across multiple applications over the next two decades. This evolutionary path would provide time for organizations to adapt while avoiding disruptive transitions that could destabilize existing technological infrastructure.

However, breakthrough scenarios remain possible, where unexpected advances in quantum hardware, quantum algorithms, or quantum applications could accelerate the quantum transition dramatically. Microsoft's topological qubit program, if successful, could provide room-temperature quantum computers with extraordinary coherence properties. Photonic quantum computing could enable quantum computers that operate using standard telecommunications infrastructure. Algorithmic breakthroughs could reveal quantum advantages for problem classes that currently seem intractable.

The convergence of artificial intelligence and quantum computing could provide another pathway to accelerated quantum development. AI systems might discover quantum algorithms that humans cannot conceive, while quantum computers might provide exponential speedups for AI training and operation. This symbiotic relationship could create rapid progress in both technologies that exceeds current projections.

Regardless of which scenario unfolds, the quantum transition will require continued international cooperation, substantial investment in quantum research and development, and thoughtful preparation for both quantum opportunities and quantum challenges. The decisions made today about quantum technology development, security preparation, and workforce development will determine how successfully our technological civilization adapts to the quantum age.

The Quantum Imperative

The quantum revolution is not something that will happen to us—it is something we are actively creating through our choices and actions. Every investment in quantum research, every quantum computing course offered at universities, every organization that begins preparing for quantum threats, and every policy decision about quantum technology development shapes the trajectory of this transformative technology.

The imperative for action is clear. Organizations that delay quantum preparation risk being left behind as quantum technologies mature and provide competitive advantages to early adopters. Nations that underinvest in quantum research and development may find themselves technologically dependent on others in an increasingly quantum-enabled world. Individuals who fail to develop quantum literacy may find themselves unprepared for careers in the quantum economy.

Yet the quantum revolution also represents unprecedented opportunities for addressing humanity's greatest challenges. Quantum computers could accelerate the development of new medicines, enable more accurate climate modeling, and optimize resource allocation in ways that benefit billions of people. Quantum technologies could provide unbreakable security for sensitive communications while enabling new forms of international cooperation and coordination.

The choice is ours: we can be passive observers of the quantum revolution, or we can be active participants in shaping a quantum future that reflects our values and serves our collective interests. The quantum age is not something that awaits us in the distant future—it is the technological landscape we are entering today.

The quantum revolution represents both the greatest technological opportunity and the most significant challenge of our time. Success in navigating this transition will require the best of human ingenuity, cooperation, and wisdom. The future belongs to those who can harness quantum computing's transformative power while managing its disruptive effects on existing technological and social systems.

As we stand at the threshold of the quantum age, we carry with us the accumulated knowledge of previous technological revolutions and the unprecedented tools that quantum technologies provide. The quantum future is not predetermined—it is ours to create. The choices we make today will determine whether the quantum revolution enhances human prosperity and capability, or whether we struggle with its transformative effects. The quantum paradigm shift has begun. The time for preparation and action is now.

Glossary

Amplitude - A complex number that determines the probability of measuring a particular quantum state. The square of the amplitude gives the probability of observing that state when measured.

Annealing (Quantum) - A quantum computing approach that finds optimal solutions by slowly evolving a quantum system from an initial state to a final state that encodes the solution to an optimization problem.

Bell State - One of four maximally entangled quantum states of two qubits. These states demonstrate the strongest possible quantum correlations between particles.

Bit - The basic unit of classical information that can be either 0 or 1. Classical computers process information using sequences of bits.

Bloch Sphere - A geometric representation of qubit states as points on the surface of a sphere, where the north and south poles represent the classical 0 and 1 states.

Coherence Time - The duration for which a quantum system maintains its quantum properties before environmental interference destroys quantum superposition and entanglement.

Decoherence - The process by which quantum systems lose their quantum properties due to interaction with the environment, causing superposition states to decay into classical states.

Entanglement - A quantum mechanical phenomenon where particles become correlated in such a way that the quantum state of one particle instantaneously affects the state of its entangled partners, regardless of distance.

Error Correction (Quantum) - Techniques for protecting quantum information from errors caused by environmental interference, typically using multiple physical qubits to encode each logical qubit.

Fault-Tolerant Quantum Computing - Quantum computation that can maintain arbitrarily low error rates by using quantum error correction, enabling indefinitely long quantum calculations.

Gate (Quantum) - Basic quantum operations that manipulate qubits, analogous to logic gates in classical computing but operating on quantum superposition states.

Grover's Algorithm - A quantum algorithm that searches unsorted databases quadratically faster than classical approaches, providing speedup for optimization and search problems.

Hadamard Gate - A quantum gate that creates superposition by rotating qubits from classical 0 or 1 states to equal probability superposition states.

Interference (Quantum) - The phenomenon where quantum states can combine constructively or destructively, enabling quantum algorithms to amplify correct answers while canceling incorrect ones.

Logical Qubit - An error-corrected qubit implemented using multiple physical qubits and quantum error correction, capable of reliable quantum operations.

NISQ (Noisy Intermediate-Scale Quantum) - The current era of quantum computing characterized by systems with 50-1000 qubits that have significant error rates but can demonstrate quantum advantages for specific problems.

No-Cloning Theorem - A fundamental principle of quantum mechanics stating that arbitrary quantum states cannot be copied perfectly, constraining quantum algorithm design.

Pauli Gates - A set of fundamental single-qubit quantum gates (X, Y, Z) that perform rotations around different axes of the Bloch sphere.

Post-Quantum Cryptography - Cryptographic algorithms designed to remain secure against attacks by both classical and quantum computers, also called quantum-resistant cryptography.

Quantum Advantage - The demonstration that a quantum computer can solve practical problems faster or better than classical computers.

Quantum Circuit - A sequence of quantum gates applied to qubits to implement quantum algorithms, representing the quantum analog of classical computer programs.

Quantum Communication - The transmission of quantum information between quantum systems, enabling applications like quantum key distribution and quantum internet.

Quantum Cryptography - Security techniques that use quantum mechanical properties to provide theoretically unbreakable encryption and secure communication.

Quantum Key Distribution (QKD) - A quantum communication protocol that uses quantum mechanical properties to detect eavesdropping and establish secure cryptographic keys.

Quantum Sensing - The use of quantum systems to measure physical quantities with precision that exceeds classical measurement capabilities.

Quantum Simulation - The use of quantum computers to model quantum systems, enabling study of molecular behavior, materials properties, and fundamental physics.

Quantum Supremacy - The demonstration that a quantum computer can perform a specific computational task exponentially faster than the best classical computers, regardless of practical utility.

Quantum Volume - A metric for quantum computer performance that accounts for the number of qubits, gate fidelity, and connectivity, providing a single measure of quantum system capability.

Qubit - The basic unit of quantum information that can exist in superposition states representing combinations of 0 and 1 simultaneously, enabling quantum computational advantages.

Shor's Algorithm - A quantum algorithm that can factor large integers exponentially faster than known classical algorithms, threatening current cryptographic security.

Superposition - A fundamental quantum mechanical principle where quantum systems can exist in combinations of multiple classical states simultaneously until measured.

Surface Code - A quantum error correction scheme that arranges qubits in a two-dimensional grid and can correct errors using only nearest-neighbor interactions between qubits.

Topological Qubit - A theoretical type of qubit that encodes quantum information in topological properties of quantum systems, potentially providing natural protection against certain types of errors.

Trapped Ion - A quantum computing approach that uses individual ions confined by electromagnetic fields as qubits, achieving high gate fidelities and long coherence times.

Universal Quantum Computing - The ability to perform any quantum computation using a finite set of quantum gates, analogous to universal classical computation.

Further Reading

Foundational Texts

Nielsen, Michael A., and Isaac L. Chuang. *Quantum Computation and Quantum Information: 10th Anniversary Edition*. Cambridge University Press, 2010. The definitive textbook on quantum computing and quantum information science, providing comprehensive coverage of both theoretical foundations and practical applications. Essential for readers seeking deep technical understanding of quantum algorithms and quantum error correction.

Mermin, N. David. *Quantum Computer Science: An Introduction*. Cambridge University Press, 2007. An accessible introduction to quantum computing designed for computer scientists and mathematicians without extensive physics backgrounds. Excellent for understanding quantum algorithms and computational complexity theory.

McMahon, David. *Quantum Computing Explained*. Wiley, 2008. A practical introduction to quantum computing concepts with worked examples and programming exercises. Particularly useful for readers interested in hands-on quantum programming experience.

Popular Science and General Interest

Ball, Philip. *Beyond Weird: Why Everything You Thought You Knew About Quantum Physics Is Different*. University of Chicago Press, 2018. A clear explanation of quantum mechanics that addresses common misconceptions while providing intuitive understanding of quantum phenomena underlying quantum computing.

Dowling, Jonathan P. *Schrödinger's Killer App: Race to Build the World's First Quantum Computer*. CRC Press, 2013. An engaging account of quantum computing development that combines technical explanation with historical narrative and humor. Excellent for understanding the broader context of quantum computing research.

Bernhardt, Chris. ***Quantum Computing: An Applied Approach*****. Springer, 2019.** A practical introduction to quantum computing that balances theoretical understanding with hands-on programming examples using current quantum computing platforms.

Quantum Algorithms and Programming

Yanofsky, Noson S., and Mirco A. Mannucci. ***Quantum Computing for Computer Scientists*****. Cambridge University Press, 2008.** A comprehensive introduction to quantum computing designed specifically for readers with computer science backgrounds, emphasizing algorithms and computational complexity.

Johnston, Eric R., Nic Harrigan, and Mercedes Gimeno-Segovia. ***Programming Quantum Computers: Essential Algorithms and Code Samples*****. O'Reilly Media, 2019.** A practical guide to quantum programming with code examples in multiple quantum programming languages. Essential for readers interested in implementing quantum algorithms.

Hidary, Jack D. ***Quantum Computing: An Applied Approach*****. Springer, 2021.** A comprehensive textbook covering quantum computing theory, algorithms, and applications with practical programming examples and exercises.

Quantum Cryptography and Security

Gisin, Nicolas, and Grégoire Ribordy. ***Quantum Cryptography*****. Reviews of Modern Physics, 2002.** A comprehensive technical review of quantum cryptography principles and implementations, essential for understanding quantum security applications.

Chen, Lily, Stephen Jordan, Yi-Kai Liu, Dustin Moody, Rene Peralta, Ray Perlner, and Daniel Smith-Tone. ***Report on Post-Quantum Cryptography*****. National Institute of Standards and Technology, 2016.** The definitive government report on post-quantum cryptography standardization efforts, essential for understanding the transition to quantum-resistant security.

Quantum Technologies and Applications

Jaeger, Lars. ***The Second Quantum Revolution: From Entanglement to Quantum Computing and Other Super-Technologies*. Springer, 2018.** A comprehensive overview of emerging quantum technologies beyond computing, including quantum sensing, quantum communication, and quantum metrology applications.

Paris, Matteo G. A., and Jaroslav Rehacek. ***Quantum State Estimation*. Springer, 2004.** A technical treatment of quantum measurement and state estimation, essential for understanding quantum sensing and metrology applications.

Business and Economic Implications

Harrow, Aram W., and Ashley Montanaro. ***Quantum Computational Supremacy*. Nature, 2017.** An important scientific paper analyzing the conditions under which quantum computers can outperform classical systems, essential for understanding quantum computing's practical potential.

Preskill, John. ***Quantum Computing in the NISQ Era and Beyond*. Quantum, 2018.** The seminal paper that defined the current era of quantum computing, essential for understanding current limitations and future prospects of quantum technologies.

Historical Perspectives

Freiberger, Paul A.*Fire in the Valley: The Making of the Personal Computer*. McGraw-Hill, 2000. While focused on classical computing, this book provides valuable perspective on how transformative technologies develop and achieve commercial success, offering insights relevant to quantum computing adoption.

Ceruzzi, Paul E. *A History of Modern Computing*. MIT Press, 2003. A comprehensive history of computing development that provides context for understanding quantum computing as the next stage in computational evolution.

Research and Professional Resources

Quantum Journal (published by Verein zur Förderung des Open Access Publizierens in den Quantenwissenschaften) An open-access journal publishing high-quality research in quantum science and technology. Essential for staying current with quantum computing research developments.

Physical Review Quantum (American Physical Society) A premier journal for quantum information science research, covering both theoretical and experimental advances in quantum computing and quantum technologies.

IBM Quantum Documentation and Tutorials Comprehensive online resources for quantum programming using IBM's quantum computing platforms, including tutorials, algorithm examples, and hardware specifications.

Microsoft Quantum Development Kit Documentation Complete documentation for Microsoft's quantum programming tools and Q# language, essential for quantum software development using Microsoft's quantum computing platform.

Google Quantum AI Publications Regular research publications from Google's quantum computing research division, providing insights into cutting-edge quantum hardware and algorithm development.

Online Courses and Educational Resources

IBM Qiskit Textbook A comprehensive online textbook covering quantum computing theory and practice using IBM's quantum programming platform. Available free online with interactive coding examples.

Microsoft Quantum Katas Self-paced tutorials and programming exercises for learning quantum computing using Microsoft's Q# language. Excellent for hands-on quantum programming experience.

Quantum Computing: An Applied Approach (EdX Course) University-level online course covering quantum computing fundamentals, algorithms, and applications. Suitable for technical audiences seeking comprehensive quantum education.

These resources provide pathways for continued learning across different levels of technical depth and areas of interest. Readers interested in quantum computing careers should prioritize the programming and algorithm resources, while those focused on business applications may find the economic and technology assessment materials most valuable.

www.ingramcontent.com/pod-product-compliance
Lightning Source LLC
LaVergne TN
LVHW022225200926
848481LV00006B/2126